THE DYNAMICS OF
MOTOR-SKILL ACQUISITION

THE

DYNAMICS

OF MOTOR-SKILL

ACQUISITION

MARGARET D. ROBB
State University of New York
College at Cortland

PRENTICE-HALL, INC., Englewood Cliffs, New Jersey

PRENTICE-HALL PHYSICAL EDUCATION SERIES

ISBN: P 0–13–222059–8
C 0–13–222067–9

Library of Congress Catalog Card Number: 70–38907

10 9 8 7 6 5 4 3 2 1

Printed in the United States of America

PRENTICE-HALL INTERNATIONAL, INC., LONDON
PRENTICE-HALL OF AUSTRALIA, PTY. LTD., SYDNEY
PRENTICE-HALL OF CANADA, LTD., TORONTO
PRENTICE-HALL OF INDIA PRIVATE LIMITED, NEW DELHI
PRENTICE-HALL OF JAPAN, INC., TOKYO

*Dedicated to my mother and father
in appreciation of their guidance
and constant encouragement*

CONTENTS

FOREWORD   *xi*

PREFACE   *xv*

CHAPTER ONE

INTRODUCTION   1

What Must Be Studied in Skill Acquisition, 2
Cybernetic Theory, 3
Summary, 4

CHAPTER TWO

LEARNING, ABILITIES, AND PERFORMANCE   6

Motor Performance and Skill Learning, 7
    Organismic Variables, 7
    Maturation and Degeneration, 8
    Task Requirements, 9
    Motivational Factors, 10
Types of Learning, 10
    Identifying Learning Classifications in Research, 11
The Measurement of Learning, 13
Individual Variance in Learning, 16

Abilities and Success, 16
　　Physical Fitness Abilities, 17
　　Specific Task Abilities, 18
　　Memory Capacities, 19
　　Perceptual Motor Abilities, 21
Summary, 21

CHAPTER THREE
THEORETICAL CONSTRUCTS OF LEARNING　　23
An Overview of Learning Theories, 24
　　Association Theories of Learning, 25
　　Cognitive Theories of Learning, 28
　　Cybernetic Theory, 30
Summary, 36

CHAPTER FOUR
UNDERSTANDING THE TERM SKILL　　38
Definitions of Skill, 38
　　Descriptive Definitions, 39
　　Operational Definitions, 39
Mechanisms of a Skilled Act, 40
Characteristics of a Skilled Act, 42
　　The Hierarchical Organization, 42
　　Executive Programs and Subroutines, 43
　　The Acquisition of Subroutines, 44
　　The Temporal Patterning of Skills, 47
Summary, 49

CHAPTER FIVE
THE STAGES OF LEARNING A SKILL　　51
Phase I: Plan Formation, 52
　　Man's Receptor Capacities and Limitations, 53
　　Man's Perceptual Capacities and Limitations, 56
　　Summary of Phase I, 59
Phase II: Practice, 60
　　Receptor Cues During Practice, 61
　　Schedules and Distribution of Practice, 62
　　Whole and Part Learning, 63

Ongoing Processing and Feedback, 64
Summary of Phase II, 66
Phase III: Automatic Execution, 66
Changing the Sequential Organization, 67
Summary of Phase III, 71
Summary, 72

CHAPTER SIX
FACTORS AFFECTING SKILL ACQUISITION   74
Retention, 74
Retention of Motor Skills, 76
Transfer of Learning, 77
Transfer and Skill Acquisition, 78
Motivation, 79
Goal Setting and Level of Aspiration, 79
Cultural Influence and Motivation, 82
Ability Grouping, 83
Task and Environment Demands, 84
Reaction and Movement Time, 86
Reaction Time, 86
Movement Time, 90
Summary, 90

CHAPTER SEVEN
FEEDBACK AND SKILL LEARNING   92
Definitions of Feedback, 93
The Role of Feedback, 94
Action and Learning Feedback, 94
Motivating Feedback, 95
Factors Affecting the Role of Feedback, 96
Feedback Loops, 100
Open and Closed Loops, 101
Internal Loops, 103
Group Interaction Feedback, 104
Noise and Feedback, 105
Reference Patterns, 106
Implications for Teaching, 108
The Future of Feedback, 111
Back to the Present, 113
Summary, 114

CHAPTER EIGHT
SPORT CLASSIFICATION SYSTEMS 116
Criteria for a Taxonomy, 117
Traditional Classification Systems, 118
Recent Taxonomies, 121
    Knapp's Continuum of Skills, 121
    Fitts's Levels of Difficulty, 129
    Vanek and Cratty's Abilities and Games Classification, 132
Summary, 134

CHAPTER NINE
THE INSTRUCTIONAL PROCESS 135
Assessing the Entering Behavior of the Student, 135
Analyzing the Task, 138
    A Classification System, 139
    Analysis of Critical Components, 141
The Role of the Teacher, 146
    Encoding Information, 147
    Mode of Practice and Training Media, 149
    Providing Feedback, 150
Assessing Terminal Performance, 151
Summary, 152

APPENDIXES AND BIBLIOGRAPHY 156
Appendix A, 156
Appendix B, 159
Bibliography, 163

INDEX 169

FOREWORD

In the preface to his 1926 book, *The Psychology of Coaching*, Coleman R. Griffith stated that the work was a product of "a psychologist's excursion into the field of athletic competition." In reverse, one might describe *The Dynamics of Motor-Skill Acquisition* as a result of a physical educator's involvement in the field of psychology, specifically that branch of psychology concerned with the study of human performance.

In Griffiths's time, it was somewhat unusual for a Professor of Educational Psychology to set forth, within the pages of a book, his views about coaching techniques. Indeed, this published study may be regarded as one of the early tangible connections between psychology and physical education. Shortly thereafter, in 1930, Clarence Edwin Ragsdale, in response to the needs of his students of psychology, prepared a manual, *The Psychology of Motor Learning*, in which he attempted to relate some of the laws and principles of learning to motor activities. This work allied Ragsdale with the concerns of physical educators although it is "How Children Learn the Motor Types of Activities," his contribution to the *Forty-Ninth Yearbook of the National Society for the Study of Education* that has become better known to motor learning theorists. That numerous scholars of human behavior since Ragsdale have been concerned with various aspects of skilled performance is well-established by the literature of psychology. Yet, few of these individuals focused their efforts on the study of skill as it occurred in the context of sport performance. Griffiths's "excursion" and the documentation of the research carried on in his special laboratory for the psychological study of men in athletic competition stood, for a comparatively long period of time, as a singular endeavor.

John D. Lawther, a psychologist whose coaching interest and success was responsible for his adoption of physical education as his career field, exemplified another individual who effectively related the study of human skill performance to the concerns of physical educators. Lawther's influence permeated the profession through his writings and in the personages of his graduate students. In particular, the 1951 publication of *Psychology of Coaching* gave teachers of skills a book that amalgamated principles of several academic disciplines with data empirically derived from coaching and other high level learning situations.

During the post–World War II years, the period in which the name of John Lawther became prominent as a motor learning expert, numerous physical educators began to direct their studies more toward the formal discipline of psychology. It became somewhat commonplace for graduate students engaged in the pursuit of advanced physical education degrees to "take a few psych courses," e.g., psychometrics, learning theory, physiological psychology, etc. The appeal to physical educators to penetrate the professional literature, emerging ideas, and modes of experimentation of psychology grew. At the same time, as a field of study, psychology was itself becoming sophisticatedly complex. New subfields were developing: personality, group dynamics, human performance, to name but a few. Obviously, the articulation of human behavior with the technological age in which we were beginning to live posed enormous challenges to scholars of the behavioral sciences. In the sense that Margaret D. Robb pursued knowledge in one of these vanguard movements within the field of psychology, her "excursion" was somewhat unique. Her association with Paul M. Fitts in "Human Performance Theory," (as he purportedly referred to it during its early conceptualization) provided her with the specific frame of reference out of which this textbook was developed.

To the writing of this book, then, Professor Robb brought a basic understanding of performing man as an information processer. Given that this theoretical grounding was imposed upon years of participation and teaching of sport and activity skills, it is understandable that *The Dynamics of Motor-Skill Acquisition* provides a highly relevant approach to one of the central concerns of physical education—the guiding of skill learning and performance.

Robb's major theme, simply stated, is that skill learning and performance must be studied as an aggregate—a collective and integrative unity of environment, individual, task, and goal. The author's commitment to the notion that the individual is the center of a network of communication and control around which all of his behavior takes place is reiterated throughout the text. In describing the information-processing functioning of man, Dr. Robb consistently draws upon examples of everyday practices in the gymnasium and on the playing field to clarify her points of emphases. Here, her rich background as a teacher of physical education skills, and perhaps more importantly, her role as a teacher of prospective skill teachers, makes it possible for her to link current psychological theory with the mundane problems of physical educators in a meaningful way.

Discussion of task analysis and stages and levels of learning reflects Margaret Robb's orientation to behavioral cybernetics. Whereas most physical education textbooks addressing the topic of skilled performance are organized primarily around the learner/performer and variables associated with the execution of the skilled act, Robb gives serious consideration to the examination of the skilled task, per se, and those aspects of behaving which unite the individual and the task: feedback and processes occurring within learning.

As a fellow student of psychology, I have shared Margaret Robb's beliefs that cybernetic theory and interpretations of man's physical behaviors hold promise for unraveling some of the mysteries of "man in motion" that have continued to escape our understanding. As a physical educator, I have been most sympathetic with Dr. Robb's desire to incorporate the knowledges derived from human performance theory into the mainstream of thought of physical education. Therefore, I regard it as a privilege to write this brief introduction to *The Dynamics of Motor-Skill Acquisition.* I mark the occasion as one in which a long needed and timely publication takes its place in the literature of physical education.

PEARL BERLIN

University of North Carolina
Greensboro, North Carolina

PREFACE

The emphasis in this book is on the cybernetic approach to understanding learning. The material was prepared primarily for physical educators interested in the dynamics of skill acquisition. Prospective teachers, as well as persons currently in the physical education profession who are interested in devising methods of instruction based on information processing theory, should find this material helpful. The material may also serve as a basis for research and study in a particular area within the total context of human performance and skill acquisition.

This book does not offer a simple solution to determining methods of instruction. Knowledge that completely explains how man learns a skill does not exist and thus this is not a "how to do it" book. Although many teachers and students want to be told *the* method to use in order to teach or acquire skill, there is no one method. Perhaps the greatest mistake teachers of teachers have made in the past is to give students the idea that there are certain methods of teaching which must be used. The rate of change in society is so fast that what works today may be obsolete tomorrow. Educators have been guilty of not allowing or encouraging students to develop their decision-making powers for the selection of methods of instruction. Contrasted to previous texts on motor learning and methods of instruction, the approach this book takes is to view man as an information processor with limitations, capacities, and adaptive qualities. It offers some information for you to process which may be helpful in understanding the complex problems involved in learning a skill and in structuring the learning environment.

One of the most difficult tasks encountered in the study of human performance and skill learning from a cybernetic approach is becoming familiar with the terminology. Throughout the text various terms are defined and explained. The book is organized in a hierarchical manner. The initial chapters provide the reader with background material concerning the learning-performance distinction, the theoretical constructs of learning, and various definitions of the term "skill" as well as words associated with skill. One of the more important areas considered is an operational definition of skill. The main advantage of an operational definition of skill is that it allows one to delineate the characteristics, properties, and mechanisms of a skilled act. Chapters one through four provide a gradual introduction to problems of skill learning as well as a basis for understanding the dynamics of skill acquisition.

Chapter five presents information concerning the *process* involved in learning a skill. Man's receptor-perceptual capacities and limitations are examined. This chapter emphasizes the *learner* and the *learning* of a skilled movement. Additional factors affecting skill acquisition, such as retention, motivation, transfer, and effector capacities, are presented in chapter six.

Feedback, the heart of the skill-learning process, is constantly referred to throughout the text. Chapter seven expands on the topic of feedback and delves more deeply into the various roles, types, modes, and future of feedback.

While the first several chapters are concerned with the learner and process of learning a skill, chapters eight and nine deal with the types of tasks to be learned and the actual instructional procedure. Several different ways of developing a task taxonomy are presented. It is recognized that each taxonomy has limitations. However, it is also recognized that each taxonomy emphasizes a different purpose: (1) to improve communication, (2) to develop curriculum material, (3) to gain a perspective or place an emphasis on certain behavioral objectives and evaluation procedures, and (4) to devise methods of instruction.

Chapter nine presents material concerned with the process of developing an instructional plan. Task variables and individual variables as well as the role of the teacher are examined. Whenever possible, examples are presented to aid in the understanding of possible outcomes resulting from the process of relating individual, task, and teacher variables.

It is extremely difficult to acknowledge properly those who have had a direct or indirect influence in the preparation of this book. The seminars with the late Paul M. Fitts and discussions with Richard Pew gave me the initial information input for the material in this book. Although the information was overwhelming at first, the "bits" of information were eventually encoded into "chunks," transformed into words, and effected on paper. The process was slow because new transformation rules had to be learned as well as old information in memory storage banks recoded. I am grateful that the learning was done in an atmosphere of mutual respect and understanding for the problems of skill learning, regardless of field. There was no prejudice or protectiveness of disciplines. For a woman, in physical education, this was indeed a delight.

I am also indebted to my colleagues and students at Cortland who indulged me by reacting to the material in this book and who may have suffered through the initial attempts. I am especially grateful to Dr. Katherine Ley, who not only encouraged the writing of this book, but who patiently made suggestions and edited the entire manuscript. She, like other effective teachers, has that quality of demanding, insisting, and inspiring others to do more than they thought they were capable of doing. Her persistent questioning and insight, together with her common sense, made her help invaluable.

When one begins to attempt to write a book there needs to be someone who has faith in the material besides the author. Dr. Pearl Berlin served as that person for this book. Her reaction to the prospectus and outline as well as her final review of the manuscript was most helpful, and I am indeed appreciative.

For you, the reader, my hope is that as you process the information in this book you will react, suggest, refute, enlarge and, in so doing, will be able to accomplish your executive plan.

M. ROBB

Cortland, New York

CHAPTER ONE

INTRODUCTION

The problems associated with how one acquires skill are numerous and complex. For that matter, the term *skill* is itself an illusive and confusing word. Physical educators are prone to use *skill* to describe the qualities of a person's motor performance. The person who has reached a certain level of proficiency may be said to be "highly skilled" or "poorly skilled." We may say a person has average skill. We describe a person as "well skilled" if he moves efficiently and effectively or if he appears to have good potential for accomplishing a specific movement.

Skill is also used in reference to specific motor tasks. When we speak of a skill, we mean an isolated performance that must be learned. The spike in volleyball and the dribble in basketball are specific skills. We say, also, that certain skills must be learned and then combined, if we are to participate in a certain game or sport. In this sense we mean a combination of several complex movements.

Everyone has attempted to perform some type of skill at one time or other; it may have been driving a car, hitting a baseball, or tying a shoe lace. All of these movements are skills which must be learned. The question logically arises, "How are these tasks learned?" The study of how people learn the movements involved in sports and dance is a concern of physical educators. Helping people learn to move efficiently and effectively in order to accomplish a specific task is one of their aims. The professional physical educator uses the modalities of sports, games, and dance in order to accomplish broad education goals.

Other professional fields also are concerned with the acquisition of skill. The surgeon must perform skilled tasks and use complex movements in an operation. The airline pilot must employ different skills to maneuver his plane successfully. The term *skill,* again, may either describe the level of proficiency acquired or may be used as a noun to inform us just what motor task the person is attempting to accomplish. One also must acquire skill in order to drive a car, read a radar scope, or strike a tennis ball.

Regardless of the meaning we intend in using the word *skill,* the interchangeable meanings make writing about the *acquisition of skill* extremely confusing. When we speak of acquiring skill, we must describe the process and the interaction of various forces encountered by an individual when he seeks to accomplish a specific task. Thus, *skill* in this context implies the accomplishment of a task and does not refer to the connotative quality of the movement.

Many hours of practice are necessary before a skilled movement is executed smoothly and efficiently. Sometimes movements are still awkward after hours of practice. The task, if accomplished at all, may be performed in a very inefficient manner. It is both interesting and curious that some persons learn to perform some movements skillfully while others seemingly cannot. Movements that can be performed skillfully differ from person to person, and no one seems able to perform all acts equally well.

WHAT MUST BE STUDIED IN SKILL ACQUISITION

The knowledge required for understanding skill acquisition comes from many sources. Physical educators must rely on their own practical experiences in helping others acquire skill in movement and sport activities. Like professionals in any other field they have the problem of applying theoretical constructs and research findings to practical skill learning problems. Findings and theories from the fields of psychology, sociology, physiology, and anthropology as well as research within the field of physical education itself enhance knowledge concerning the acquisition of skill. Physical educators tend to seek research that is immediately applicable. Most researchers realize this is not always possible, and the discovery of knowledge, although it is not *immediately* applicable, is extremely important.

The role of the researcher in any field is to discover new knowledge and facts as well as to test innovations and present practices. The educator's role is to apply the findings from sound research; he has the difficult task of determining the most suitable methods of instruction. Methods or techniques for the improvement of learning are discovered through research, through invention, and through innovation. An innovation may be the result of trial and error, observation, and more trial and error. Some innovations grow out of sheer desperation. In any case, it is the role of the teacher-researcher to test the soundness of innovations.

The teacher of physical education must draw on knowledge from various basic disciplines and must utilize experimentation and invention within his own field.

Criticism has been leveled at teachers who do not read or apply research findings. It is easy to understand why teachers become disenchanted with research findings—the research literature is inundated with contradictory results. If more application is to occur, a fresh approach is needed. The theoretical background of an emerging science called *cybernetics* may provide this fresh approach to understanding man and the regulation of movement.

CYBERNETIC THEORY

The field of cybernetics as applied to the study of human behavior is based on the premise that an analogy can be drawn between human behavior and servomechanisms. Servomechanisms are self-regulating devices used in machines which make use of the principle of feedback. For example, a thermostat, a guided missile, a steering wheel, or a boat rudder are self-regulating devices which affect future performance of the particular equipment involved. Human behavior resembles the servomechanisms principle in that feedback from past experience aids in determining future behavior.

Man basically is an information processing system. He uses his memory capacity, makes decisions, and executes simple and complex skills. If we are to begin to understand how certain complex tasks (such as are involved in sports, medicine, industry, etc.) are learned, it is vital to consider how man processes information and regulates behavior. The field which investigates man's control and regulation of his environment is termed *human performance*. The field of human performance is concerned with man as a processer of information and deals with the topics of sensory, perceptual, and effector processes. Man's capabilities, limitations, and integrative qualities are studied in order to improve the structure of the environmental situation and thus shorten the learning process.

Interest in the study of human performance was renewed by psychologists during World War II because of the urgent need to train men in short periods of time. Men were needed to perform highly technical movements, such as flying airplanes, shooting guns, and detecting blips on a radar screen. The "older" methods of trial and error learning did not suffice.

The research and experimentation conducted at this time were the beginning of the application of findings to the acquisition of sport skills. These investigations stimulated further research and experimentation in the area of motor-skill learning.

Weiner (1961) considered the entire field of control and communication theory in relation to both machines and animals, and termed the study of this field *cybernetics.*

Weiner and his associates first used the term cybernetics. Terminology of existing theories on the control and/or regulation of movement and behavior was too biased. The word *cybernetics* is derived from the Greek word *kybernetike,* which, literally translated, means the "art of steersmanship." Smith and Smith (1966) pointed out that the study of learning must be based on an understanding of the "sensory-feedback" organization of behavior. Feedback is an extremely important concept in cybernetics.

Cybernetics per se is *not* a theory of automatic machines or electronics. The science of cybernetics does not imply an "inhuman" treatment of man or that man is synonymous with machines. Connotations of the word *cybernetics* are varied and subjective. However, misuse of the word is similar to value judgments applied to teaching machines. Many educators believed the use of teaching machines implied the elimination of the teacher. These fears were unfounded. Technology does not automatically imply the inhuman use of humans. No doubt, telephones, automobiles, airplanes, and printing machines were feared by some when they were first introduced. Man is an extremely complex organism. While computers can perform many intricate operations, only man is capable of making decisions. Computers are not capable of "self-regulation"; man is. The study of computers has proven helpful in identifying principles that aid in explaining man's behavior and learning characteristics.

The premise proposed in this text is that problems of skill execution are mainly perceptual problems rather than motor problems. Perceptual problems are those concerned with the processing, interpretation, and use of sensory stimuli. Man is viewed as an information processer with capabilities of self-regulation.

SUMMARY

Each person concerned with the learning process—whether he be the student learning a skill, the researcher testing new ideas and/or theories, the educator applying principles from theories and research, or the teacher determining methods of instruction and structuring the environmental learning situation—will find the theory and science of cybernetics helpful for a more complete understanding of the complexities involved in skill acquisition.

Each of us has experienced the confusion and frustration of learning a skill. Cybernetics, through its terminology and analogy to the principles and construct of operation of an automated computer can aid us in our continuing investigation of man's behavior while acquiring skill.

The dynamics of motor-skill acquisition begin with the study of man himself—his capabilities, his limitations, and his operational characteristics. This knowledge together with an awareness of task components aids in the structuring of the learning environment.

CHAPTER TWO

LEARNING, ABILITIES, AND PERFORMANCE

The term *learning*, although commonly used, is a complicated word that has many ramifications. The student of skill acquisition must examine the many aspects of skill and the factors related to skill learning before he can begin to understand the process and interpret the results.

Skills are learned. Much of what is known about learning has been extrapolated from research on subhumans. Man's learning process differs from that of animals. Basing conclusions about man's behavioral characteristics from knowledge gained in animal studies may be dangerous and misleading. Our concern here is with learning as a *human* function.

Humans vary in their abilities to learn. These individual differences are a vital consideration in the total learning environment. Not all individuals begin their learning at the same place in the skill continuum, and the rate at which they progress differs correspondingly.

Learning encompasses a wide range of behavior, and the only way we can be certain that learning has occurred is to observe and/or measure the change in behavior. This change in behavior is reflected in a change in performance. However, a change in performance does not always indicate that learning has taken place. An outstanding performance may occur once and never be duplicated. Learning implies a change in behavior which is more or less permanent. Therefore, we measure the *retention* of a certain behavior.

While some variables have a primary effect on skill learning, others affect motor performance. The distinction between the terms *skill learn-*

ing and *motor performance* is necessary for a thorough understanding of skill acquisition.

MOTOR PERFORMANCE AND SKILL LEARNING

The term *motor,* when used with the term *performance,* implies an effector action, a physical action, or an action requiring the use of large-muscle groups. Performance can be temporary in nature, and the term *motor performance* refers to an effector action which may not be permanently "fixed" in an individual's movement repertoire.

The term *skill,* as used with the term *learning,* implies a reorganization of basic patterns of movement resulting in a permanent change in effector behavior. *Skill learning* refers to a change in effector behavior which occurs as a result of practice. The resultant change in behavior will continue to be evident with each repetition of the skill, and is, therefore, consistent and more or less permanent.

The execution of a skilled task can be altered by certain learning variables. Among the variables that primarily affect skill learning are feedback, retention, schedules of practice, and transfer. Motor performance is affected by other variables, such as organismic factors, maturation or degeneration, task requirements, and motivational factors. Each of these can greatly affect one's performance on a task.

It is sometimes difficult to distinguish learning variables from performance variables. Variables which affect a temporary change in behavior cannot be attributed to learning. Learning continues over a long period of time and may be slow in manifesting itself. Outwardly it may appear that an individual has learned little, when in fact, improvement is gradually occurring. The total performance of the individual must be considered before determining how much he has learned. The distinction between learning and performance variables enables the teacher to improve the structure of the learning environment and to be aware of what is happening to the student. Methods of teaching, as well as techniques of evaluation, may be more wisely determined because of an understanding of the terms, skill learning and motor performance.

The following descriptions and examples of performance variables and behavior changes will help to clarify the distinction between the terms *skill learning* and *motor performance.*

ORGANISMIC VARIABLES

Organismic variables are related to the physical functioning of an individual. Increases in cardiovascular endurance, flexibility, or strength are organismic variables which affect performance. A performer who goes into training can change his physical functioning and thus improve his performance. By the same token, the individual who allows himself to get out of shape will find his performance deteriorating quickly.

Suppose a student wishes to throw a ball as far as possible. He knows the basic throwing pattern, but he wishes to increase the distance he can throw the ball. He may accomplish his objective by increasing his arm and shoulder strength or by reorganizing his throwing pattern. If the distance he can throw is increased because of an increase in strength, the improvement is due to an organismic variable. If, on the other hand, the increase is due to some change in the basic movement pattern, it can be attributed to skill learning.

Following earlier reasoning, an increase in the distance one can throw a ball may or may not be the result of learning. In this case the thrower must first increase his flexibility in order to extend his range of motion (organismic variable); then he must learn a different throwing pattern in order to utilize the increase in range and flexibility. He has improved his performance and has also learned.

If an individual changes the distance he can throw a ball because of an increase in knowledge, e.g., he learns to release the ball at a 45° angle to increase the distance, this change can be attributed to learning. One may know the best angle of release is 45°, but if he is unable to re-lease at that precise angle, there is no evidence of his knowing or having learned the principle, unless a written test is given.

The physical educator who considers physical fitness the primary objective of physical education and the teacher who places great emphasis on improvement in performance are particularly concerned with organis-mic variables. The individual in poor physical condition due to illness or neglect cannot improve very quickly within the span of time allotted to sport units. This type of person is at a disadvantage to the person who is physically well and will need a greater span of time for practice. As a general rule, the highly skilled, physically conditioned person can per-form well with little practice—a very discouraging prospect for the stu-dent who lacks experience, skills, or physical conditioning, and yet must be compared to the skilled student.

MATURATION AND DEGENERATION

As a child matures, he acquires the ability to use various muscular systems that affect his performance. He cannot perform many skilled movements until he has matured sufficiently. A child cannot ride a bicycle until his legs have grown long enough to reach the pedals. He cannot catch balls until his hand-eye coordination develops. Principles of growth and development are important in understanding changes in performance. The importance of early experiences in movement patterns which prepare the child to learn skills cannot be emphasized enough.

Beyond a certain age, performance generally deteriorates. In some cases this change in performance can be directly related to a change in the organismic condition of the individual. Thus, the variable of degeneration, and the variables of growth and development, are directly related to motor performance.

TASK REQUIREMENTS

The specific requirements of a particular task affect the performance of that task. The type of equipment used by the performer, the limits imposed by rules, and the conditions of play, including weather, crowds, and officials, are examples of task requirements that influence the execution of a skill.

There are innumerable examples of the influence of equipment on the requirements for performing a task. Equipment that is ill-fitting, in unsafe condition, improper in weight, etc., hinders good performance. Improved modern equipment has had beneficial effects. New pole vault records, set with the use of the fiberglass pole, reflect the changes in task requirements. In skiing, metal or fiberglass material used in construction of skiis, the addition of steel edges to wooden skiis, lamination of wood and metal, and variation in length, weight, and flexibility each necessitate a change in performance.

Equally important are changes imposed by rules and conditions of play. Athletes who were familiar with collegiate basketball rules performed differently when they competed in international contests under international rules. Women track performers had to modify their performance when the distance to be run in various races was changed. Imagine what changes in performance would be required if basketball backboards were raised to twelve feet from the floor or tennis nets were four feet high instead of their present height!

Any such change in performance is attributed to a change in task requirements. However, a person who changes from one type of equipment or condition to another, such as from wooden to metal skiis, makes adjustments in his movement pattern that are more or less permanent. In this sense, such a change can be attributed to learning, but the major change is due to the change in the performance variable.

MOTIVATIONAL FACTORS

Motivation or desire is a vital prerequisite to learning and performance. If a person is not motivated to learn, learning will not take place; a person who is not motivated will not perform well. "He could have been a champion if he wanted to, but he was not 'hungry' enough" or "they were the 'underdogs' going into the tournament and really wanted to win," are statements which reflect man's ability to respond to added challenge and to excel if desire is present. Numerous records have been broken and new marks set because of man's great desire to excel. Many times an individual has broken a record with a spectacular performance he is unable to repeat. Coaches recognize that desire or motivation can make a person of average skill excel. Motivation, therefore, affects both immediate motor performance and the more permanent learning process. (Motivation as a factor affecting skill learning is discussed in Chapter 6.)

TYPES OF LEARNING

Traditionally learning is divided into three categories: (1) cognitive, (2) affective, and (3) effective learning. Although each category can be distinguished by the kind of learning achieved or the area most influenced, the process which underlies all types of learning appears to be the same. This point of view was expressed by Bilodeau and Bilodeau (1961) in their summary of motor-skill learning research. They used the term *motor-skill learning* for convenience in classifying research and did not mean that motor-skill learning is different from other types of learning.

Fitts, commented on the process involved in the various types of learning as follows:

> Processes which underly skilled perceptual-motor performance are basically very similar to those processes which underlie language behavior as well as processes involved in problem solving, concept formation, etc. If so, then laws of learning should be similar. . . distinctions between verbal and motor processes serve no special purpose.[1]

Cognitive learning refers to changes in the behavior of a person in the areas of problem solving, concept formation, reasoning, and acquisition of knowledge through memory and/or understanding. Cognitive learning deals with conscious awareness and involves the mental processes associated with thinking.

[1] P. M. Fitts, "Perceptual-Motor Skill Learning," *Categories of Human Learning,* ed. A. W. Melton (New York: Academic Press, 1964), p. 243.

Affective learning applies to attitudinal changes. While attitudes may be changed through facts or knowledge associated with cognitive learning, the resultant change in behavior relates to the value structure of the individual. For this reason, affective learning is probably the most difficult to accomplish in adults.

Affective learning is dependent upon environmental factors. Such influences as home, friends, and surroundings, both past and present, are difficult to counteract, so attitudinal changes occur very slowly. Attitudes can be changed at all ages, but the older a person becomes, the less likely he is to change his attitudes. As a person ages, a longer period of time and more constant influence is needed to effect an attitudinal change.

Attitudinal changes are the most difficult to measure because the learner can easily demonstrate the "expected behavior" whether or not he intends to behave that way again. Studies of attitudes and affective learning outnumber those of other types of learning and are among the most popular in physical education research.

The area of *effective learning* relates specifically to the motor output of an individual. Categorically speaking, the acquisition of physical skill or motor learning is classified as effective learning. Just as affective learning is associated with cognitive learning, effective learning also involves with cognitive learning. Cognitive and effective learning require some physical act to prove that learning has taken place. The learner must speak, write, move, or perform some physical act to communicate what he thinks, understands, believes or knows.

IDENTIFYING LEARNING CLASSIFICATIONS IN RESEARCH

Anyone pursuing a study of learning, and specifically, skill learning, must be able to determine the appropriate label for learning research studies. Accurate classification is essential in order to make adequate interpretations of research. Knowing whether a study was done in the context of cognitive, affective, or effective learning affords greater insight in interpreting research.

The type of learning being investigated can be determined by identifying the *dependent* variable in the study. This can generally be accomplished by asking, "What is the primary means used by the experimenter to determine a change in behavior?" In studying the effect of something (known as the experimental variable) on something else (known as the dependent variable), it is essential to control or minimize other factors or variables in order to rule out their effects on the dependent variable. Only in this way can the true effect of the experimental variable be determined. For example, if a study researches the effect of practice upon some type of movement pattern (the dependent variable), it is concerned with effective learning.

Movement patterns involved may be either fine or gross muscular movements. Fine motor movements involve intricate and small adjustments in behavior such as flipping switches, pushing buttons, or other such movements of the hands. Large or gross movements are those in which the body moves through space and uses the large muscle groups of the body.

Physical educators tend to be critical of effective learning studies that have utilized only fine motor movements while psychologists are inclined to utilize fine motor coordinations in laboratory studies. To evaluate the relative merits of using gross motor movements as opposed to fine motor responses, the number of variables involved in the study must be considered. Anything that might influence the performance of a gross motor skill should be identified. Strength, for example, has an important effect on the performance of a gross motor skill. The major reason for using fine motor responses in learning research could be to eliminate the effect of strength on the results of the study.

As a general rule, studies labeled "motor-skill learning" require the subjects to perform tasks that involve some type of non-verbal movement. Thus, the dependent variable is motor in nature, and the independent variable is of a non-verbal variety. Flying an airplane, manipulating large equipment, learning a sport skill, and performing gross movements are examples of tasks used in the study of motor-skill learning, i.e., the effective domain.

Studies dealing with the affective or attitudinal domain of learning involve a different type of dependent variable; e.g., a subject's relation to a group as measured by a sociogram, the reaction to group dynamic techniques, or responses to terms such as honesty, sportsmanship, or the teaching of a particular subject. The latter example includes physical education studies of students' attitudes toward physical education and their reactions toward a particular type of course or program. The effectiveness of a course offering is often judged by the results of such studies.

The cognitive domain includes those studies in which learning is measured by a verbal or written response that indicates the amount, quality, scope or depth of intellectual achievement. Various achievement examinations, analogy tests, college entrance tests, etc., are tools that measure cognitive learning.

Man's skills are affected by his attitudes, his values, and his knowledge, as well as by his physical capabilities, but it is important to remember that the *process* of learning, or how learning takes place, is apparently the same regardless of the *type* of learning.

THE MEASUREMENT OF LEARNING

Progress in learning is measured by recording changes in performance. The changes may be assessed in a variety of ways, some of which are regarded as objective measures and others which are known as subjective evaluations. In the majority of research studies credence has been given to those studies which utilize only objective measures. Where subjective techniques had to be used because objective measuring tools were not available, the studies have been considered "second class" by many, even though researchers utilized all available procedures to quantify the data as objectively as possible.

Studies in which the results are graphed are commonly reported in research literature. The response for each trial over a specified period of time are plotted on a graph. The resulting curve shows the progress of learning and is called a *learning curve.*

Figure 1 is an example of a learning curve. As can be seen, at the ninth trial the curve leveled off. This leveling off is called an *asymptote.* When an asymptote occurs in the plotting of a learning curve, some educational experimenters refer to it as a *plateau* in learning.

The reason for the occurrence of a plateau has concerned educators greatly. Does the plateau indicate that learning has stopped? Is there a

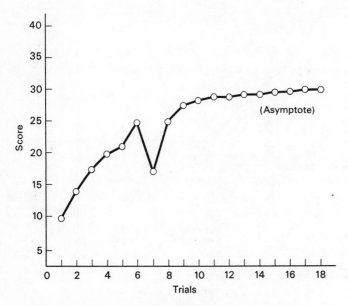

FIG. 1.   Sample Learning Curve Showing an Asymptote

"leveling off" period in all types of learning or does an asymptote appear because of the influence of other factors? Does the learning phase end and the influence of other factors cause the performance curve to rise again?

Some educators believe a plateau occurs when motivation to learn is lowered. Others believe the plateau is directly related to the learning process, and that it implies a *discontinuity* in learning.

Evidence contradicting the hypothesis that plateaus indicate a discontinuity in learning was presented by Crossman (1959). Crossman studied data on employees who had worked as cigar rollers for seven years. Figure 2 shows that over this period of time, the workers continued to improve and increase the number of items produced. The expected plateau or asymptote did not occur. Even after performing the same task of rolling cigars for seven years, the workers had not attained peak

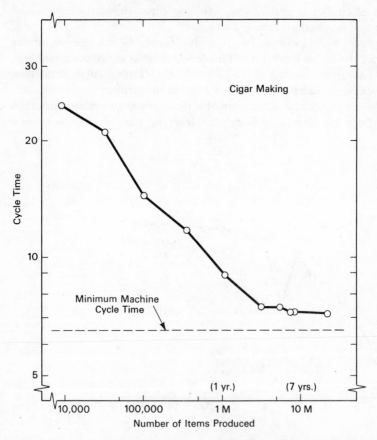

FIG. 2. DATA FROM CROSSMAN, 1959. ILLUSTRATION OF IMPROVEMENT IN SKILL OVER A LONG PERIOD OF TIME

learning capacity. The only leveling off occurred when the machinery involved limited production.

It seems safe to assume that individuals rarely reach the limits of their capacity to learn. If plateaus do occur in learning curves, they must be due to variables other than learning capacity. These variables are: (1) inadequate motivation, (2) fatigue, (3) lack of a precise measuring instrument, or (4) environmental restrictions.

The evidence presented by Crossman (see Figure 2) suggests that learning will continue over a long period of time provided the learner continues to be motivated. Barring environmental restrictions, learning continues indefinitely, possibly to the extent that an individual's full capacity for learning is never reached.

Many persons have difficulty accepting this line of reasoning, because it is difficult to determine the capacity of each individual. No one has been able to devise a means of accurately measuring or even estimating the innate capacity of an individual to learn or to perform. Although the term *motor capacity* appears in physical education literature, it is equally difficult to determine the capacity of an individual to learn motor tasks and/or to perform motor skills. We may think we know the physiological capacity of man, and yet performance records are broken (the four minute mile and the seventeen foot pole vault). In such feats, however, performance is being increased. The term motor capacity in some cases denotes a combination of learning and performing; i.e., an individual's motor capacity may be his capacity to learn plus his physiological and physical capacity to perform.

In attempting to devise accurate methods of measuring learning capacity, experts have been concerned with procedures for making subjective evaluations as objective as possible. Subjective evaluations are the preliminary steps to the development of appropriate measuring devices. Therefore, learning to express subjective evaluations in numerical units so that they can be given statistical treatment is imperative.

Many educators are of the opinion that there are some important educational achievements that are not measurable at all, especially in the area of affective learning. In identifying these, they must consider the question, "What important achievements cannot be observed as to their presence or absence?" If an achievement can be recognized as being present, and its presence can be verified by other observers, it must be present. If an achievement cannot be identified as present, its very existence, as well as its importance, must be questioned.

The fact that the degree of presence cannot now be measured does not mean that it can never be measured. It simply means we have not yet discovered or developed the tools needed for measurement. Physical educators must devote more time and energy to the study and exploration of techniques for quantifying achievement if they wish to substantiate accomplishments in areas that they have tended to classify as unmeasurable, but have claimed as objectives. Such affective factors as sportsmanship, teamwork, and similar behavior manifestations fall into this area.

INDIVIDUAL VARIANCE IN LEARNING

The discussion above required a consideration of the problem of individual differences. Educators have long been aware of the existence of individual variance and have given lip service to the need to consider individual differences in designing learning experiences. Only recently have we begun to understand something about some of the human factors that may cause the normal range of variation. Previously, we concentrated on atypical learning patterns or disabilities. The knowledge gained from such sources and the improvements in handling and utilizing data, enable a closer study of variations within the normal range. The limitations and capacities of man will be discussed in greater detail later; all that need be said at this point is that individuals do vary in the capabilities they bring to the learning situation.

When the learning of a specific task is initiated, certain questions arise about the learning process that will be demonstrated by individuals in the group. Are they more likely to be similar or different in their *rate* of learning? Does practice on a specified task reduce the amount of individual variance or increase it?

Evidence from research studies points out that when the motor task is complex, variance among individuals increases with practice. As individuals continue to practice a complex motor task, the variation between individuals in the group becomes greater. The group that may have been homogeneous at the start is likely to increase in heterogeneity.

Thus, we can explain why group instruction is more valuable during the initial stages of learning than during the later stages. As practice continues, the variance within the group becomes greater, and individual instruction becomes more desirable and is more beneficial to the learner. The explanation is that the learning rate and learning capabilities vary for each individual. As individuals practice, each person apparently progresses at his own rate.

ABILITIES AND SUCCESS

The role played by man's receptor, perceptual, and effector capacities and limitations is extremely important in the understanding of skill acquisition. Human performance theorists study man's capacities and limitations in an effort to learn the answers to questions, such as "How much can man remember? Process? Attend to?" Physical educators view man's capacities in terms of his motor abilities.

MOTOR ABILITIES. The term *ability* is defined as "a fairly enduring trait or characteristic." *Motor ability* refers to enduring traits or characteristics that affect an individual's effector or output qualities. While some abilities are inherited, others are the result of early experience and environmental exposure. Specific motor abilities examined by various researchers have been kinesthetic sense, balance, eye-hand coordination, and gross body movements. It is questionable whether a "general" motor ability trait exists. Although some athletes appear to be proficient in many sports, the existence of a so-called "natural athlete" is doubtful. Athletic success in several sports is probably due to the similar patterns of movement used in many of our sports.

Basic movement patterns are necessary prerequisities for many sport tasks. For this reason it is important for boys and girls to learn as many fundamental movements as possible in pre-adult life. Running, skipping, hopping, jumping, and walking are fundamental locomotor movements. The individual who has acquired a wide variety of movement patterns in early life is most likely to be able to execute complex movement patterns in later years.

PHYSICAL FITNESS ABILITIES

Physical fitness is a term frequently used to indicate the organismic condition of an individual and affects performance. Fleishman (1966) and his associates investigated more than sixty different types of fitness tests and compiled the following list of eight physical fitness abilities under the term "motor fitness":

Extent Flexibility. Ability to flex or stretch the trunk and back muscles as far as possible in a forward, lateral, or backward direction.

Dynamic Flexibility. The ability to make repeated, rapid flexing movements in which the resiliency of the muscles in recovery from the strain or distortion is critical.

Static Strength. The maximum force which a subject can exert, for a brief period, where the force is exerted continuously up to this maximum. In contrast to other strength factors, this is the force which can be exerted against external objects (e.g., lifting heavy weights, pulling against a dynamometer), rather than in supporting or propelling the body's own weight.

Trunk Strength. This is a second, more limited, dynamic strength factor specific to the trunk muscles, particularly the abdominal muscles.

Gross Body Coordination. Ability to coordinate the simultaneous actions of different parts of the body while making gross body movements.

Gross Body Equilibrium. The ability of an individual to maintain his equilibrium, despite forces pulling him off balance, where he has to depend mainly on nonvisual (e.g., vestibular and kinesthetic) cues. Although also measured by balance tests conducted with the eyes closed.

Stamina. The capacity to continue maximum effort requiring prolonged exertion over time. This factor has the alternate name of cardiovascular endurance.

Dynamic Strength. The ability to exert muscular force repeatedly or continuously over time. It represents muscular endurance and emphasizes the resistance of the muscles to fatigue. The common emphasis of tests measuring this factor is on the power of the muscles to propel, support, or move the body repeatedly or to support it for prolonged periods.[2]

Knowledge about the physical fitness components which an individual possesses should help to predict his success in tasks involving or requiring a high degree of fitness. If a high relationship or correlation exists between endurance components and certain track events, we predict the eventual success an individual can achieve on the basis of his ability to withstand prolonged physical activity.

SPECIFIC TASK ABILITIES

As learning progresses, a specific factor related to the task may play a determining role in eventual success. Successful learning requires the appropriate use of selected abilities at the appropriate time. During specific stages of learning, certain abilities seem to play a more important role than others. For example, verbal understanding may be more important in the initial or early stages of learning a skill than in the later stages. This ability must be available at the required time for learning to progress properly.

A study by Fleishman and Hempel (1955) showed that an ability *specific* to the task was more important for success as practice progressed. Thus, in the particular task used in this study, during the early stages of practice, spatial characteristics appeared to be the chief contributor to individual differences in success. Later in learning, abilities more specific to the task appeared to be more important.

Fleishman (1966) also generalized that certain *combinations* of abilities contribute to successful learning of tasks at various stages of

2 E. A. Fleishman, "Human Abilities and the Acquisition of Skill," *Acquisition of Skill*, ed. E. A. Bilodeau (New York: Academic Press, 1966), pp. 156–57.

learning. For example non-motor abilities such as verbalizing may play a more important role in the early learning stages while later in learning, task-related factors may play the vital role.

MEMORY CAPACITIES

How man remembers is of extreme importance in the eventual success of executing a skill. Waugh and Norman (1965) have suggested that man has a primary and secondary memory system. According to their model all items (stimuli) enter the primary memory where they are either forgotten or rehearsed. If rehearsal occurs, the items may enter the secondary memory bank. Melton (1963), on the other hand, has argued for a theoretical structure which explains memory capacity to be a short term and long term memory system which operates on a continuum and actually consists of a single storage mechanism.

Short term memory refers to a person's capacity to remember a certain number of objects immediately after presentation. A person can usually repeat a series of numbers immediately after they are presented. After waiting for a period of time, however, the numbers may or may not be remembered. If they are remembered, it is because they have been delegated to the long term storage or secondary system. Rehearsal affects one's ability to store and hence, recall material. Forgetting does occur from non-use, but the activity which goes on during the interval between learning and recall greatly affects retention. If one is allowed to rehearse the numbers without interfering activity, it is more likely that he will retain the numbers.

The amount of material to be learned is directly related to the short term memory capacity. There is no clear-cut evidence as to how the short term memory operates. Short term memory is tested by immediate recall which prevents rehearsal or recoding of materials. If a longer interval is present before recall, the materials to be learned can be rehearsed or recoded and sent to the long term storage system. The memory span for short term storage has been investigated by Miller (1956). He suggested that the "magic number," seven, plus or minus two represents the amount of information or storage capacity of the short term memory system. However, man is able to remember more items than seven plus or minus two because he has the ability to recode material and delegate it to long term storage. We recode by "chunking" the material or by putting it into larger categories. Thus, the amount of the material to be learned is greatly affected by the coding capacity or the capacity of the individual to "chunk" material. It may well be that short term storage has a limited capacity and that only four to six items can be remembered without the aid of rehearsal or recoding. However, since man has the capacity to rehearse and/or recode he is able to remember more items.

The ability to recode material is related to the meaningfulness of the material. If the learner can see no relationship between the material to be learned and his already existing chunking categories, then he is not likely to remember the material. He has not "perceived" the material because it holds little meaning for him.

Meaningfulness also involves recognition by the performer that there will be a future re-use of the material learned. This relates to students' demands for relevancy of learning. Memorizing a phone number that will never be used holds no relevancy for the learner, especially if he knows he can look it up in a phone book. Likewise, memorizing the pounds of pressure in a volleyball is meaningless if the student believes he is unlikely to have to put air into a volleyball. Thus, the learner will memorize this fact for recall on a test, but since it loses relevancy after the test, he will no doubt forget it.

The total length of practice time also appears to aid the individual's retention because meaningful practice helps the individual increase the "chunks" of material learned. Repeated experience allows the individual to learn ways in which the sequential organization of the movement pattern is arranged. He is then able to deal with incoming information in larger units.

Since what is remembered is the result of a person's interpretation of the stimuli presented, practice allows a refinement and correction of interpretations. The memory does not store the actual information received by the senses, but rather, our perception of the data. Thus, practice with feedback allows one to test the accuracy of perception with the real world.

It may well be that we retain novel or fresh information simply because we perceive it. That is, the sense organs relay the information to the central processing system because it is "something that caught our eye." Actual retention of the novel information depends upon the rehearsal of this material and the encoding of it in long term storage. We may also retain novel information because we become interested in it and are thereby motivated to process the information and to remember it.

Purdy and Lockhart (1962) found some indication that initial performance in a gross motor skill is a valuable index to future performance and, hence, retention. The higher the initial level of skill, the greater the retention because the material is more highly organized and, therefore, more firmly fixed in the long term storage system. Thus, it is extremely difficult to forget how to ride a bicycle because the total organization of the movement pattern has been refined over many practice trials. Level of proficiency may be related to retention because of the high level of organization of the receptor-feedback-effector processes. Once a person becomes proficient at performing a skill, it is doubtful that he will forget it.

PERCEPTUAL-MOTOR ABILITIES

Briefly, the term *perception* means the interpretation of sensory stimuli. *Perceptual-motor abilities* refer to the capability of an individual to process, interpret, and use sensory stimuli for performing some type of task.

Certain abilities which affect proficiency in motor output and are related to perceptual-motor learning are labeled as *perceptual-motor abilities.* The ability to discriminate between figure and ground, for example, involves the interpretation of the input. If a child cannot *perceive* a ball from the background of the floor he will have extreme difficulty catching the ball. The individual's capacity for figure-ground discrimination may be deficient and must be developed before he can proceed with learning. The child must learn to attend to selected sensory information before he can begin the process of sensory integration and eventual successful effector action.

Perceptual abilities also deal with such things as processing information through encoding, decoding, and decision making. The term *encode* refers to the categorization of sensory information. Encoding utilizes information in storage (memory). Through a process of scanning, man categorizes and/or recognizes information input.

After the information is retrieved from the sensory storage system, or *decoded,* a decision must be made which regulates the act or output. Man's ability to make decisions is an extremely complicated process. Briefly, man makes decisions based upon previous experiences, new information, and the predicted consequences of the act. Memory ability is limited, and many times decisions are based on limited retrieval of past events. Recognizing this limitation of man leads to the conclusion that one of the values of computers is the information storage capacity. Man's decisions, would perhaps be more effective and efficient if he did not always rely on his relatively "poor" memory ability.

SUMMARY

In this chapter the terms learning and performance have been examined. Learning is a more or less permanent change in behavior and is measured by recording response changes. While limitations to learning are determined genetically, man seemingly has a vast capacity to learn.

Progress in learning a task is determined by a change in the performance of a person on that particular task. It is important to realize that while *skills* are learned, the *performance* of a task can be affected by variables other than those associated with learning. For this reason, it is important that the teacher understand the distinction between learning and performance.

In most discussions about learning it is necessary to divide the topic in some reasonable way to facilitate the explanation. This is true of any topic as complex and interrelated as the learning process. Traditionally, learning has been differentiated into three subtopics for convenience of discussion. The actual process involved appears to be the same whether the learning is in the cognitive, affective, or effective domain.

The study of learning can be approached in several different ways. Learning may be studied by determining the rate of learning and graphing the progress made, as in a learning curve. Differences in the rate of learning between individuals may be investigated, as well as individual responses to different methods of teaching. It is also possible to compare the mean behavior of one group to the mean behavior of a similar but different group.

A sound interpretation of learning studies is often difficult because it is necessary to differentiate between factors that are innate and those that are the result of environment, practice, experience, and personality. An interpretation of a study can easily be deficient if it has failed to recognize and allow for individual differences between subjects.

Individuals vary in their abilities to perform a task. Some individuals apparently have learned or inherited certain qualities which aid them in acquiring success while others must compensate for a lack of ability specific to the task.

All teachers are familiar with the statement "education must allow for individual differences." While no one would deny it, one often wonders how to deal effectively with a large class of individuals. As practice continues, individual variance increases and the use of specific techniques to aid individuals is necessary. The teacher is also faced with the problem of determining commonalities among students and of predicting eventual success in learning. Certain abilities play more important roles at various stages of the learning process. Abilities are fairly enduring traits or characteristics and play a different role depending on the stage of learning.

Almost all behavior is motor in nature. Man responds with voluntary and involuntary movements. This response reflects an individual's reaction to the perception of selected stimuli. The study of skill learning is the study of the process of how such selection takes place.

CHAPTER THREE

THEORETICAL CONSTRUCTS OF LEARNING

Theories are usually developed through experimentation and offer a general explanation of how or why something occurs. Theories are developed from hypotheses. An hypothesis is a *tentative* theory proposed by an investigator as a provisional explanation of how or why something occurs. Once the hypothesis is stated, the researcher proceeds to devise and perform an experiment that will either support or refute the hypothesis. Since research is conducted in an orderly fashion whereby as many variables (influences) as possible are controlled, general knowledge about the soundness of the hypothesis is gathered.

An hypothesis must be subjected to experimentation in many ways and from many different approaches. Hypotheses that continue to be acceptable or supported become theories. If a theory can stand-up under additional testing, careful scrutiny, and in-depth investigation, it becomes a law, i.e., a rule of conduct. Principles are more like laws than hypotheses. They have been subjected to experimentation and have stood the test of time.

In recent years research investigators have begun using the term *model* as a means of testing theories. A model is a tentative explanation of *how* something occurs. Although a model is generally displayed by a schematic "block" drawing, verbal descriptions, in the form of analogies, have also been used to explain certain phenomena.

A model may be said to be a theoretical "operating code." This means that minor modifications or variations can be made in it whenever additional information or experimentation deems it advisable. A model seems to be more easily modified or varied than a theory, perhaps because the emphasis is on the function or operation of something. Because it is often concerned with process, a model may involve a "flow" of action or may indicate a direction to an ordering of occurrences, as in a block diagram.

Psychologists studying learning have professed many learning theories; however, knowledge which completely explains how man learns does not exist. Instead, "islands" of knowledge concerning man's learning process have been identified, some of which have resulted in the formulation of theoretical constructs or models. Learning theories form the basis for a total understanding of the dynamics of skill acquisition because skills are learned.

Learning theories are classified into three broad categories. These categories are: (1) association, (2) cognitive, and (3) cybernetic. Association theorists stress the significance of responses the organism makes and the *association* or *connection* of the response to the stimuli. They emphasize the role of prior experience and the reinforcement of responses.

Cognitive psychologists believe that learning is a process through which the learner discovers and understands relationships. Sensory experiences aroused by the external situation are organized into meaningful significance. Learning results from a change in the way one perceives his environment as the result of insight.

Cybernetics is a new area or theoretical construct which also attempts to explain man's learning behavior. Cybernetic theorists do not entirely discount the experimental findings of other learning theories. Instead, they embrace ideas and findings from many theories and attempt to examine these findings from a computerized viewpoint. Cybernetic theory also attempts to explain the intricate workings of the brain and learning by comparing the mechanics and operation of the nervous system to that of complex electronic computers.

Feedback is an extremely important aspect of the learning situation in cybernetic theory. It is much more than a form of reinforcement or mere knowledge of results. Feedback is recognized in cybernetic theory as *error information* and is one of the more important variables controlling and regulating human behavior.

AN OVERVIEW OF LEARNING THEORIES

The meaning and implications of various theories of learning should be clarified to help teachers to communicate with and understand students and, at the same time, help them improve their style of teaching. Methods of teaching are derived from the theoretical structure that is developed when a theoretical explanation of how learning takes place is offered. Methods of teaching sport skills are generally based on a combination of association and cognitive laws of learning. These, together with expert judgment and/or educated guesses, have provided teachers with methods of instruction.

Singer (1968) used Hilgard's term *functionalism* to describe an eclectic point of view held by many teachers of physical education. The functionalist uses insight and ideas from both cognitive and association learning theory, depending on which idea seems to produce the desired results. Thus, the person teaching badminton may use the ideas of trial and error practice to teach basic skills, and the ideas of the cognitive approach to help the student learn the strategy of the game. This might be termed a *pragmatic* approach to teaching since those ideas and principles which "work" are applied to the actual teaching of skills.

For each learning theory various names, branches, or hybrid ideas have developed. Association type theory has been termed bond theory, connectionism, trial and error, or stimulus-response by some. Cognitive type learning theorists have used names and ideas from Gestalt psychology, holistic psychology, and phenomenal psychology. Cybernetic theory is associated with such terms as human performance, information processing, and self-regulatory experimentation.

ASSOCIATION THEORIES OF LEARNING

Some experimenters who have contributed to association learning theories are Thorndike, Watson, Guthrie, and Skinner. Association theorists, or behaviorists, believe that *habits* are the key to discovering what is learned. In order to understand how habits are acquired, a study must be made of (1) what precedes performance, (2) the performance itself, and (3) the consequences of performance.

A *stimulus* always precedes performance. Stimuli can arise from various internal sources. Organic sensations or stimuli, such as hunger pangs, are termed *interoceptors*. Sensations originating from the actions of the body itself are called *proprioceptors*. These include the muscles, tendons, and joints, which aid in determining movements and positions of the body segments. Stimuli that originate outside the organism, or *exteroceptors,* are particularly important in association theories.

Association theorists not only attempt to designate the sensory area where stimuli originate, but also believe it is important to measure the stimuli intensity. For example, the amount of light stimuli can be measured in foot-candles; auditory stimuli can be measured in decibels; and hunger pangs can be measured in terms of the number of days of deprivation. Some stimuli can be measured more easily than others, but in order to carry out successful experiments, association theorists attempt to measure carefully all stimuli, as well as designate the sensory areas affected by the stimuli.

The reaction to a stimulus is termed a *response*. Responses can be highly complex or quite simple. A complex response might be the execution of a dive, while a simple response would be pushing a button to turn off a light stimulus. In some cases the response becomes the stimulus for the next response. Thus, the term *response-produced stimulus* is used. When a response-produced stimulus occurs, there appears to be a "chaining" of stimulus-response units, which form the basis for learning.

Responses can be measured by several different methods. The simplest and most direct measurement is to count the number of times a correct response occurs. The "correct" response is determined by the criteria of the task as set by the experimenter. The number of times a response occurs is labeled the *frequency* of response. Another type of measure frequently used is the amount of time elapsed before the response is elicited. This type of measurement is termed the *latency* of response. In some cases the speed of response or total response time is measured.

A consequence of performance follows the response. At this time a reward or reinforcement can be introduced. In animal research the reward is usually some type of food pellet or other means of reducing a physiological need. In the case of humans it is not always clear how the learner will interpret the reward offered. Thus, associationists have argued that a reward is not always necessary for learning to take place. Instead, it is believed that learning takes place when the stimulus and response occur simultaneously.

The term *contiguity learning* is used when an association or connection results from the frequent simultaneous occurrence of a stimulus and a response. Associationists believe that although reward will aid the association to proceed more rapidly and will, perhaps, strengthen the connection, an association will occur, regardless of reward, if the stimulus and the response are contiguous.

In association theory, *conditioning* is an important phenomenon. There are two types of conditioning, classical and operant. In classical conditioning, a response which occurs naturally at the reflex level is paired with a stimulus which does not automatically call forth the normal response but which will eventually elicit the response with conditioning and practice. Thus, a neutral stimulus, after being paired with an adequate stimulus, can actually elicit the response which previously was elicited only by the adequate stimulus. The most famous experiment in classical conditioning was conducted by Pavlov with dogs.

In operant conditioning a response occurs without any prompting by a specific stimulus imposed by the experimenter. When the desired response occurs, it is reinforced. This increases the likelihood of that response occurring when the stimulus is presented. The response, of course, must be within the repertoire of the animal or human. Pigeons, for example, have been taught to play a game resembling table tennis through operant conditioning. When they pecked the ping pong ball, the action was reinforced with food pellets. Repeated reinforcement caused the pigeons to continue pecking or batting the ball.

Just as responses can be conditioned, they can also be extinguished by lack of reinforcement. Thus, to "break" a bad habit the reinforcement is withdrawn.

The main point of emphasis in the association theory is that the development of a unit or bond between a stimulus and a response increases the probability that the response will occur when the stimulus is presented. Complex habits are built up through a chaining of such stimulus-response units. Concepts are learned after many corrections and reinforcements.

Thorndike's famous laws of learning are based upon the principles of association theory. The law of exercise stated that repetition strengthens connections between stimuli and responses and increases the probability of a response being elicited. The law of effect emphasized the importance of reward. Responses followed by a satisfying reinforcement are more apt to be strengthened. In the law of readiness, Thorndike stressed motivation or the importance of the learner being "ready" to learn. He also maintained that learning takes place through trial and error, and that practice is extremely important.

Behaviorists or association theorists believe that people behave in response to the forces exerted upon them. In all behavior there is always both a response and a stimulus. The unit of behavior is the S-R bond. Critics of associationist's views have pointed out that if behavior is a result of forces exerted upon people, then learning is a matter of manipulating the forces exerted upon the learner. In order to use this theory effectively, someone must know how people *should* behave if we assume there is a proper response. Then the teacher or experimenter, assuming he knows the proper response, must connect it to a stimulus in order to change behavior.

Teachers who use the principles and laws of association theory subscribe to the idea that drill and habit establishment are very important elements of every lesson. The learner must practice in order to learn. Although some trial and error is permitted, the associationist teacher seeks to prevent the formation of "bad" habits. Considerable correction of techniques of execution occurs during early learning experiences in an effort to have students learn the "right way" or the "best way." A great deal of emphasis is placed on the "correct form," but learning the correct response is not necessarily accompanied by understanding.

The tennis teacher, for example, who applied the learning theory of associationism would favor drills on the forehand, backhand, and serve before playing a game. Constant practice with reinforcement would be very important. The teacher's role would be to arrange the stimuli, or situation, in order to elicit a correct response from the student. After the appropriate responses had been made to a bouncing ball, the student would be permitted to use the skills in a game.

Important in all theories of learning is the explanation of how transfer takes place. That is, what do we learn in other situations that helps us in a new situation? From the associationist point of view, transfer takes place only if the elements in one situation are identical to the elements in another situation. Learning is specific, and elements which are the same in one sport will transfer to another sport. There is no generalized pattern of transfer.

COGNITIVE THEORIES OF LEARNING

Proponents of cognitive learning theories include psychologists such as Tolman, Lewin, Combs, Snygg, and Rogers, as well as others. In answer to the question "What is learned?" cognitive theorists reply that *cognitive structures* are learned. The word perception is frequently used to explain how the learner gains meaningful relationships in order to solve problems.

These theorists have not accepted the S-R bond as the most satisfactory behavioral unit. They deny that conditioning or mechanical association of stimulus and response is applicable in understanding human behavior. Rather, the process of perception or the interpretation of sensory stimuli and the organization and reorganization of experiences best explain the regulation of behavior.

Cognitive theorists assume that displayed behavior is always appropriate to a person's phenomenal field. Combs and Snygg (1949) defined the phenomenal field as the individual and his universe, as perceived by the individual at the instant of behavior. They further postulated that all behavior is determined by, and appropriate to, the phenominal field as perceived by the behaver.

Behavior is a result of how things seem to the person. This is different from S-R or association theory which stresses behavior as the result of a stimuli or force to which a person is exposed. In cognitive theory the ultimate control of behavior always lies within the cognitive structure of the person.

Learning takes place through insight. Man, because he is the most intelligent organism, is most likely to achieve insight. Insight is aided by the organized arrangement of the environment into structural patterns. Some arrangements appear to promote insight more favorably than others. Processes inherent in the person, the interaction of the organism and the environment, and, to some extent, past experiences must be taken into account. Understanding the situation is extremely important. Thus, insight is possible only if the learning situation is arranged in such a way as to aid the learner in perceiving all the necessary aspects of the situation. In a good learning situation the problem is so structured that significant features are perceived in proper relationships, and distracting or confusing features are subordinated. Insight leads to the solution of problems. The teacher is constantly helping the student structure problems in order to gain insight or perceive the solution.

Fumbling and searching are preliminary to insight. This is more than the trial and error permitted by associationists. Instead, according to cognitive theorists, it is purposeful experimentation. The learner must understand the problem to be solved and must use a scientific approach to learning.

Of considerable interest to cognitive theorists is the *self-concept.* According to the perceptual view, people behave so that they may preserve and/or enhance their self-concepts. The self-concept is related to the perceptual field in that a learner accepts into his field anything which helps preserve and/or enhance this concept.

An individual's perception of himself depends upon (1) the nature of the physical organism he possesses, (2) the length of time he has lived, (3) the experiences he has had, (4) the operation of his current need (people perceive what they need to perceive), (5) the goals and values the individual holds.

Learning, therefore, is a problem of helping people to perceive differently. Classroom atmosphere, pacing of materials, group discussion, etc., are methods emphasized by teachers who subscribe to a cognitive theory of learning. Personal meaning in learning is also very important. Proponents of cognitive theories believe that the problems of education stem not from a lack of supplying information and facts, but from a lack of helping people to perceive differently.

Cognitive theorists explain transfer of learning differently from association theorists. Transfer, according to cognitive theory, takes place because of similar patterns. Once tasks have been learned with understanding, repeated challenges with new tasks result in progressive improvement in performance. Cognitive proponents would emphasize the learning of principles, concepts, and understandings rather than of facts and response generalization.

Information given through verbal means, such as lectures, for example, gives students raw material for filling in gaps in their perceptual fields. Words are effective for learning only if they "upset" or disrupt the perceptual field. In this way learning takes place when the field is so disorganized that a new perception is sought as a means of restoring and enhancing the perceptual field.

The teacher's role in cognitive learning is to determine the student's goal. The student is free to explore and express his own perception of the situation without fear of humiliation or reprisal. The teacher arranges the situation so that the student will have a better opportunity to solve a problem without direct instruction as to the "correct" response. In some cases, cognitive theorists believe there is no "correct" response suitable for all situations. The teacher helps to disrupt the student's field which the student must then perceive differently and reorganize.

Rogers (1956) stated that the emphasis in cognitive theory is on the *process* rather than on a manipulation of forces. Goals are value oriented. According to Rogers cognitive theorists:

> . . . value man as a process of becoming, as a process of achieving worth and dignity through development of his potentialities; the individual human being (is valued) as a self actualizing process. . . .[1]

Cognitive theorists emphasize the "self actualizing process"; i.e., helping persons to become adequate, functioning individuals is the purpose of education and hence, learning. People are always in the "process of becoming." Thus, education is an on-going affair with life.

CYBERNETIC THEORY

The emphasis in cybernetic theory is upon man's total performance capacities, limitations, and adaptive qualities. The proponents of cybernetic theory do not ignore the environmental information received by the individual and the resulting responses. They are interested in the way environmental information received from the external and internal stimuli is coded by the sense organs into patterns of neural energy and in the final motor response that results. These are the vital components in the study of man.

Whereas association theorists believe the behavioral unit of study is the stimulus-response bond, and cognitive theorists emphasize the perceptual structure, cybernetic theorists emphasize the feedback loop as the fundamental building block of the nervous system. As Wiener (1961) and others have pointed out the term *feedback* is not new. Wiener cited

---

[1] Carl Rogers and B. F. Skinner, "Some Issues Concerning the Control of Human Behavior," *Science* 124, no. 3231 (November 30, 1956): 1063.

an article published by Clerk Maxwell in 1868 in which the principle of feedback was discussed. Today there is a renewed and growing awareness of the power and importance of the feedback principle.

It is interesting to note the commonality that exists among the various theories. According to Mowrer (1960) the law of effect may be said to have postulated the principle of feedback. Cybernetic theory and the idea of self-regulatory movement carry the law of effect one step further. The law of effect emphasizes behavior modification because of the *effect of reinforcement*. Although one type of feedback can provide reinforcement, there are several types of feedback. The feedback or *servo* principle implies that an organism's behavior is automatically controlled, regulated, and adapted in a way that is of utmost importance to continued existence. In other words, the principle of feedback infers that an organism's response is the result of feedback from previous responses. Thus it is not practice that makes perfect, but rather, it is practice with *appropriate feedback* that makes perfect. The importance of this principle is implicit within the cybernetic viewpoint.

According to Annett (1969) the law of effect has been rejected both on empirical and logical grounds as the central principle of learning. The law of effect states that we repeat pleasing or satisfying experiences. We can challenge this by raising the question "How many students would like to repeat a course in which they have received A's?" The experience must have been satisfying, but generally speaking, human beings prefer to use the learning from one experience as a stepping stone to new challenges.

While associationists have described the brain as a passive digital computer which receives stimulus and plugs into the specific pathway, cybernetic theorists picture the brain as an information processing system with a large storage capacity and complex strategies or programs. Mowrer (1960) commented on the acceptance of such relatively recent developments in learning theory as follows:

> Because we have been so accustomed to think about behavior in terms of the mechanics of the 19th century, it is difficult to assimilate the implications of the new conceptions suggested by the 20th century mechanical and electronic 'control systems,' but these, as a little study will show, are vastly more relevant to the understanding of the behavior of living organisms than are the 'push button' models of the earlier day.[2]

British researchers, Welford, Bartlett, and Goody, conducted studies which led to much of the information contained in the cybernetic theories of learning. K. U. Smith at the University of Wisconsin has done

[2] O. H. Mowrer, *Learning Theory and the Symbolic Process* (New York: John Wiley & Sons, 1960), p. 12.

a tremendous amount of research in behavioral cybernetics. Welford (1951) conducted research on older workers in industry and noted that motor goals are reached in many ways. He found that while skill may deteriorate, output may remain unchanged because the worker will find new ways to accomplish the same task. Hellebrandt (1958) suggested that a memory engram is laid down when a task is learned, but that when the task is executed repeatedly the same combination of muscles are not used each time. Nevertheless, the same results can be reached despite the variety of ways of performing the task.

CYBERNETIC MODELS OF BEHAVIOR. Cybernetic theory is sometimes described by models. A model is an analogy which aids in the general understanding of a theory. In the case of cybernetic theory, three models, suggested by Fitts (1964), appear to best describe man's learning behavior. These three models are (1) a communication model, (2) a control system model, and (3) a composite model.

Communication Model

In a communication model man's behavior is conceived to be an "information-processing" activity guided by a central plan or goal. In terms of motor behavior or skill acquisition, man processes information concerning the total execution of the motor skill. Contrasted to association theories which conceive of learning as the connection of a series of stimulus-response units, a communication model views learning as the processing of external and internal information in relationship to the total plan or goal.

A communication model describes learning in the following manner. Information arrives through the receptors and is coded or transformed into symbols by the central processing system. Listening to someone talk is a form of information processing. Learning to talk involves the learning of symbolic codes. When someone converses with you, you process information by symbolic coding. The information is translated and either stored in the memory system or directed to the output area.

Psychologists working in the area of communication models have developed a theory called *information theory* in which the amount of information transmitted can be objectively measured. The term *bits* of information is used to specify the quantity of information. Bits are transformed through symbolic coding into *chunks* of information. The term *chunk* refers to several bits of information which have been organized into a meaningful group. Such grouping of information into larger categories or chunks enables man to retain more information.

The coding of information and the sequential measurement of information are concerns of cybernetic theorists. The storage system "holds" the chunks of materials. Thus, a person can soon learn to remember more and more information if he is able to code incoming stimuli, and delegate this data to the proper chunk or category. We generally do not store bits of information but we store in terms of organized perceptual chunks.

Learning problems may involve the inability of a person to properly organize chunks of material. For example, poor ability to understand may involve the lack of categorical background information with which to process incoming data.

In another example, students generally find it very difficult to remember isolated bits of information. The less important the bit seems to be, the more likely the student is to label it "trivia" or "irrelevant." Only as the bits are combined into meaningful chunks is information likely to be retained.

The ideas from communication models are helpful in understanding why problems of skill execution may be perceptual problems rather than motor problems. When a normal functioning human being (normal in the sense that his motor units are working) has difficulty executing a skilled movement pattern, we must look to the perceptual or central processing mechanisms to determine the difficulty. In cybernetic terms, the individual may not be learning the movement pattern because he is not processing the necessary sensory information, or he is not translating it effectively, or he does not have a storage chunk system which allows him to categorize the information correctly.

Using the communication model in a school situation, the teacher transmits information for the student to process. The teacher also questions the student to determine what information is being processed. What information is the learner actually seeing, hearing, or coding? When one asks a student what he is trying to do, it is not surprising to find that often he is processing the incorrect information.

Ask a beginning bowler what type of ball (hook, back-up, etc.) he just rolled and often he cannot tell you. In other words, he did not process any information regarding the action of the ball which he saw rolling down the lane. If he is asked what type of ball he was trying to roll, he may not have sufficient storage systems by which to identify and describe the type of ball rolled. Only after a series of questions and practice will a beginning bowler learn to "perceive" ball's action.

Control Systems Model

The theoretical construct or model of a control system is related to the control and/or the direction of behavior. There are two types of control systems (1) a regulator system and (2) a follow-up system.

A regulator system is characterized by a fixed goal or a fixed input, this is analagous to the temperature or thermostat control on a furnace. Once the temperature is "set," the operation of the furnace is controlled by this setting.

Maintaining an erect posture requires the use of a regulator system. When a baby is learning to walk in an upright position, he is establishing the thermostatic control. He walks a step or two and sits down. The process continues until he can walk across the room. After the upright position is "set," the body adjusts automatically to keep itself upright. When balance is disturbed or the body position is changed, the anti-gravity controls go into action without the individual having to think about how to right himself.

A follow-up system has no fixed goal or input and changes as behavior changes. Such systems are also termed adaptive systems. While a regulator system implies a static and unchanging behavioral model, an adaptive system implies an unstable system.

Man appears to operate as both a follow-up system and a regulator system. His large aim or goal is governed by the behavior of regulator system. However, man also adapts and changes his goal through experience. If the goal or aim is fixed, the person attempts to regulate output or behavior to correspond with the goal. If man determines he is not achieving his goal, he sometimes changes it.

Three processes take place when man either regulates his behavior to achieve his goal or changes his goal. These processes are: (1) the detection of progress by sampling, (2) the diagnosis of attainment of goal, and (3) the modification of responses or goal. Man samples information periodically in order to measure his progress toward his goal. Due to his great adaptability, man can quickly modify his response if he determines from his sample that he is not going to achieve his goal.

Control models are directly related to motivation and level of aspiration which are discussed in Chapter 6.

A Composite Model

Fitts (1964) proposed a third model which took into account both the ideas from control and communication models. This composite model is especially applicable to skill learning problems, as well as other learning areas.

Man learns to perform a skill through information processing, as well as through selected controls of behavior. Viewing the learning of motor skills as a composite of communication control, data processing activities, and perceptual qualities allows skill acquisition to be described in terms of the sequence of events, the temporal and spatial patterning, and the feedback function.

A composite model takes into account man's operational characteristics. In describing these characteristics, human performance and cybernetic theorists have investigated areas such as the hierarchical organization of behavior, the channel capacity for processing sensory information, and feedback loops. Each of these areas deals with hypotheses and descriptions of man's total organization of behavior.

THE HIERARCHICAL ORGANIZATION OF BEHAVIOR. Man organizes and directs behavior through a multiple level or hierarchical system. The lower levels of behavior are controlled by the upper level. The cortex is the higher level which receives and stores information, as well as gives commands.

It may be easier to conceptualize the idea of a multiple level system if we examine the performance of walking. In walking, a person is certainly not conscious of directing performance. Yet, purposeful movement does occur. According to the multiple level hypothesis, the brain monitors and directs the walk; the actual movements, including the maintenance of an upright position, are carried out by the lower centers that know their job so well they need no direct help from the higher centers. Suppose a person stumbles over a stone. Automatically he catches himself; then he becomes aware of the obstacle and realizes he nearly fell. In other words, the lower centers take care of the correction, and the higher centers become aware of the correction after it has occurred.

This is similar to the general who commands well-trained foot soldiers. They carry out the order with his help and direction and respond automatically as trained.

THE SINGLE CHANNEL HYPOTHESIS. In considering the processing of sensory information, proponents of the single channel hypothesis believe that the central mechanism allows a person to attend to only one stimulus event at a time. A second event arriving at the same time will be disregarded or held up to wait its turn until the channel is clear for it to be processed. Perhaps the old adage about "a one-track mind" holds some truth for everyone.

Experiments concerned with multiplexing or the ability to perform two tasks at the same time have been conducted to test the single channel hypothesis. We have learned from these experiments that the ability to do two things at the same time is not due to a multiple channel mechanism, but instead due to an overlearning of one of the tasks, which enables a person to divide his attention between two tasks. Thus, the hierarchical behavioral system of man and the question of a single or multiple channel for the processing of information are directly related. Man learns many tasks well, and those tasks that are learned well enough are relegated to a lower level. The apparent ability of man to perform two tasks at the same time is due to the fact that one task is executed by a lower center while the newer task is controlled by the higher center. Man cannot deal with or perform several *new* tasks at the same time.

These models can be directly applied to the teaching of sports skills. Students too often complain, "There are too many things to remember." Teachers complain that students do not listen well enough, or that students fail to pay close attention to instructions they are being given. According to cybernetic theorists, the fault is likely to be with the teacher, who offers too much new information for processing at one time. Teachers should transmit only one major, relevant chunk of information at a time. Good coaches, for example, concentrate on making the most important adjustment that will improve performance. Beginning teachers, generally, have not mastered the arts of selecting the most important thing to teach first or of transmitting one correction at a time. For that matter, the majority of teachers of *beginning* students find it extremely difficult to restrict the amount of information given, especially if they are imbued with the desire to prevent error, which is not compatible with the single channel hypothesis.

SUMMARY

The grouping of knowledge and experimental information concerning learning into theoretical constructs helps us to understand how man learns and behaves. Theories of learning greatly affect teaching methods. Teachers of physical education have generally operated as functionalists or pragmatists. The reason for basing practice on "what works" is related to the fact that no theory of learning completely explains how man actually learns.

While associationists believe that the bond between the stimulus and response is the important area of concern in understanding learning behavior, cognitive theorists are interested in perception, and cybernetic theorists are interested in determining models that describe man's behavior with the use of computer terminology.

The terms used by cybernetic theorists involve such phrases as single or multiple level, channel capacity, and feedback. Man's behavioral characteristics are described as a single channel system, operating at multiple levels, and involving regulator and additional follow-up systems. A person unfamiliar wtih computer language will have a difficult time ascertaining the meaning of the previous sentence. The terminology in cybernetic theory is particularly useful because it's newness eliminates previous bias associated with older terms used in studying the learning behavior of man.

The results of studies conducted in one theoretical construct or model cannot necessarily be generalized to explain learning as defined or theorized in another area. It is also dangerous and misleading to draw conclusions from a single experiment concerned with learning, or even from a series of experiments, and to generalize the results to explain *all* learning. Experiments conducted to refute or promote certain theoretical positions may or may not lend themselves to all theories.

CHAPTER FOUR

UNDERSTANDING THE TERM SKILL

One of the most commonly used terms in physical education is the word *skill*. We speak of a skilled person, basic skills, perceptual skills, motor skills, and skilled responses. Each of us has watched a golfer sink a putt, a basketball player shoot a basket, a swimmer glide smoothly through the water in a series of stunts or strokes, or a hurdler run gracefully over the obstacles in his path. As we watched such performances we may have marvelled at the high degree of skill displayed by the athlete, but what do we mean by *skill?* Everyone applies his or her own definitions and connotations to the term. In some cases the word and variations of it are used as though everyone agreed on the definition. However, the word *skill* has many definitions and uses.

DEFINITIONS OF SKILL

Skill can be defined from two viewpoints. One viewpoint includes definitions from a *descriptive* perspective, the other viewpoint includes definitions from an *operational* perspective.

Descriptive definitions are goal oriented and ascertain the accomplishment of specified tasks. They focus on a description of how an individual behaves while attaining a specified goal. Briefly, descriptive definitions ask, "How was the goal attained?"

Operational definitions deal with the *mechanisms* and *qualities* of a skilled act. They consider the temporal and spatial patterning of the mechanisms involved in the execution of a skilled movement. The terminology of cybernetics is especially useful in arriving at an operational definition of skill because the capacities and limitations of the receptor-effector-feedback mechanisms are examined, as well as the total organizational behavior of man.

DESCRIPTIVE DEFINITIONS

Physical educators have made a practice of defining skill from a descriptive point of view because physical education skills are generally taught by describing what is to be done, how it is to be done, and the results for which the performer should strive. Knapp (1963) used a descriptive definition of skill when she pointed out that skill is learned, and that it denotes the ability to bring about predetermined results with maximum certainty. She also mentioned that there is a minimum outlay of time and energy in performing a skill. Cratty (1964) stated that a motor skill may be termed a reasonably complex motor performance. Having acquired skill denotes that some learning has taken place and that a smoothing or integration of behavior has resulted.

From a broad, descriptive viewpoint, skill is the completion of a task with ease and precision. While the task can be physical or mental, one generally thinks of skill as some type of manipulative proficiency. A skilled movement is one in which a predetermined objective is accomplished with maximum efficiency and a minimum outlay of energy. A skillful movement does not just happen. There must be conscious effort and purposeful practice on the part of the performer in order to execute a skill.

Descriptive definitions stress one important point: the execution of the skill comes about through learning. An individual's abilities may aid him in performing the skill. Nevertheless, the organization of new patterns of movement is a result of learning. Descriptive definitions generally emphasize that skill is a voluntary movement involving the coordination of muscles in the execution of a purposeful act.

A descriptive definition of skill lacks precision and seems to concentrate on empirical evidence of its presence or absence. Of equal concern is the fact that the degree of skill attained is based largely on subjective judgment.

OPERATIONAL DEFINITIONS

An operational definition of skill is useful for a more complete understanding of the entire act of learning and performing a movement.

Any effort to define a skilled act in operational terms requires the examination of the mechanisms involved.

In one of the most complete operational definitions of skill Fitts defined a skilled response as:

> . . . one in which the receptor-effector-feedback processes are highly organized, both spatially and temporally. The central problem for the study of skill is how such organization or patterning takes place or comes about.[1]

This statement by Fitts gives a clue to the usefulness of an operational definition of skill. The interplay of the receptor-effector-feedback mechanisms and the uniformities in the patterning or sequence of activities are important processes to study. When executing a skilled act in sports, the performer successfully integrates the sequence of actions and is constantly utilizing and translating information from the senses to the effectors. The spatial-temporal organization is also effective. That is, the quarterback in football uses the information from the environment, draws on past data, and translates incoming data to effect a completed pass. He also utilizes feedback and effectively organizes the sequence of activities. In this case the skilled act requires spatial awareness as well as temporal organization for a well-executed performance.

If one accepts Fitts' operational definition, the term *skill* indicates the importance of the perceptual qualities, sensory input, and effector action. In regard to the incorrect emphasis on muscle groups implied by the label "motor skill," Fitts commented:

> The matter of what muscle groups are involved in a particular behavioral sequence is quite incidental and certainly no more important than the question of which retinal elements or which segments of the basilar membrane are involved in detecting a stimulus pattern.[2]

MECHANISMS OF A SKILLED ACT

The operational definition of Fitts stressed the mechanisms involved in skilled performances. Figure 3 presents a diagram of the mechanisms of the receptor-effector-feedback processes.

Also shown in Figure 3 is the central processing system which processes information from the external and internal environment, that is, the receptors. The receptors are the auditory, visual, olfactory, tactual, and proprioceptor sense organs. Information from the external environ-

---

[1] P. M. Fitts, "Perceptual-Motor Learning," *Categories of Human Learning*, ed. Arthur W. Melton (New York: Academic Press, 1964), p. 244.
[2] *Ibid.*

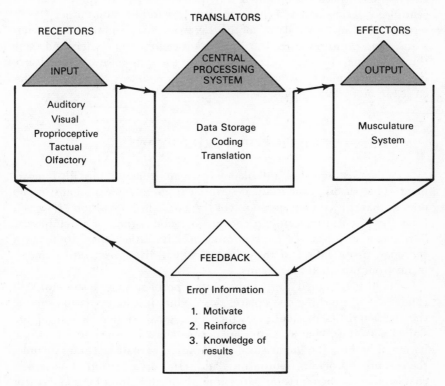

FIG. 3. MECHANISMS INVOLVED IN EXECUTING A SKILL

ment is received through the five senses of seeing, hearing, smelling, touching, and tasting. Information from the internal environment is received through the proprioceptors. Whereas association theorists have termed receptors as stimuli, cybernetic theorists term receptors *input information*.

Only a few years ago the brain was conceived as a switchboard or memory drum. At present the cybernetic theorists think in computor terms; i.e., the brain codes and organizes information into categories, stores information and data, and translates incoming information for the effectors.

The effectors are the muscles of the entire muscular system. Many physical educators have concentrated their efforts in this area in attempting to improve skill. However, as can be seen from the diagram in Figure 3, the entire receptor-effector-feedback mechanism must be considered in the total understanding of skill acquisition.

Feedback is error information, or information regarding how the effectors have performed, which is sent back to the receptors and the central processing system. Feedback, according to Fitts and Posner (1967), serves three functions: (1) to motivate, (2) to change immediate performance, and (3) to reinforce learning. In order to better understand these three functions, the section concerned with the difference between learning and performance (Chapter 2) should be reviewed. Feedback is discussed in more detail in Chapter 7.

CHARACTERISTICS OF A SKILLED ACT

What distinguishes a skilled movement from an unskilled movement? The person prone to use descriptive terminology would answer, no doubt, that the skilled person looks good. This definition, however, leads the physical educator to encourage "good form," or to emphasize how someone looks while performing a skill rather than to make a thorough investigation of the qualities which distinguish skilled movements from unskilled movements.

As Fitts is quoted above, "the central problem for the study of skill is how . . . patterning takes place. . . ." Thus, it is necessary to examine the characteristics or qualities which distinguish skilled acts from unskilled acts. Two characteristics are particularly appropriate for examination. The first, the hierarchical organization of skill learning, includes the executive program, subroutines, and serial organization. The second characteristic is the temporal patterning or coordination of the movement pattern.

Each characteristic of a skilled movement, as opposed to an unskilled movement, lends itself to be defined in operational terms. Understanding the qualities of a skilled act is especially important for the physical educator who must understand the problems involved in skill acquisition and for the learner who is trying to become skilled.

THE HIERARCHICAL ORGANIZATION

As previously stated, cybernetic theorists believe man's control of behavior is organized as a multiple level process. It follows that a skilled act is learned through a hierarchical organization and is organized in a hierarchical manner. An unskilled act lacks this type of organization.

One can best conceive of the term *hierarchy* by thinking in terms of an organizational chart in which the president of the executive board is at the top, with officers of various subunits and members at lower levels. The president and the executive board direct and delegate responsibilities to the lower units.

Miller, Galanter, and Pribram (1960) used the term Plan to imply the hierarchical nature of behavioral organization. A Plan, as defined by Miller, et al., is "the process through which the organization controls the order in which a sequence of operations is performed."[3] The concept of a hierarchical organization of behavior is based on the assumption that all skilled acts must be considered in relation to a purpose or *plan,* as well as the actual execution.

Bryan and Harter (1899) first presented evidence of the hierarchical nature of a skilled act. They conducted an experiment in learning the intricate coding system of the Morse Code. They observed that their subjects used conscious control as they studied each individual code during the first stages of learning. During later acquisition of the telegraphic skill, subjects were able to group codes or letters. Eventually the act of sending a message became largely automatic. Thus, the subjects had a *plan.* As the *plan* was accomplished, certain acts were delegated to a lower level.

The student who is learning a skill must deal with several intricate movements or segments. Some of the movement patterns may have been acquired through previous experience and practice and may already have been delegated to a lower level. Any new movements or combinations of movements will require the attention of the central processing system, i.e., higher levels. In the learning of a skilled task, various segments of the task must become automatic and be delegated to a lower center. Once certain segments of the task can be handled at lower levels, the central processing system is free to deal with additional requirements of the task.

EXECUTIVE PROGRAMS AND SUBROUTINES

Instead of using the term Plan as Miller, et al., suggested, the terms *executive program* and *subroutines* will be employed here to permit a better understanding of the hierarchical organization of skill. The executive program is the overall purpose or plan of the act, while subroutines are units of movement which, after they have been overlearned, can be delegated to a lower level. They are those movements which eventually become largely automatic. In other words, a skill is directed by an executive plan and certain subroutines form the patterns of movements by which the executive plan is carried out.

Executive programs can further be distinguished by defining their mode of operation. What are executive programs capable of doing? What distinguishes an executive program from a subroutine? Executive plans serve as follows: (1) they provide an overall logic or give direction to the

[3] G. A. Miller, E. Galanter, and K. Pribram, *Plans and the Structure of Behavior* (New York: Henry Holt and Company, 1960), p. 16. Reprinted by permission.

skilled movement; (2) they order the execution of certain subroutines; (3) they make decisions and adaptations and are quite flexible in nature; and (4) they act as a goal, aim, or objective.

Subroutines may be thought of as parts, or more or less isolated units of the total executive program. Instead of being flexible and adaptable, subroutines are fixed and run off automatically once the sequence is established. They exhibit characteristics which allow them to be repeated over and over again unless interrupted or changed by the executive plan.

An illustration of one type of executive program is the crawl stroke in swimming. The total program includes the subroutines of the kick, arm strokes, and breathing. The final skilled act requires an executive plan for ordering the various subroutines, i.e., the sequential execution and coordination of those subroutines that must work in relation one to another.

There is some danger that the illustration of the crawl stroke implies that the execution of a skilled act requires merely the chaining of one activity to the next. The integration of units, or subroutines, is much more complicated than that of chaining as suggested by associationists. As Lashley (1951) pointed out, "The order must be imposed upon the motor elements of some organization other than direct associative connections between them. . . ."[4]

Executive plan usually depends upon the execution of several subroutines. A repeated skill is never performed identically with each performance. Rather, the same effect or executive plan can be achieved in several ways. The skilled person, however, has narrowed the range of variations to within the subroutines he uses to accomplish the task. The beginner or unskilled person, on the other hand, is inclined to employ greater variability; and, sometimes uses more subroutines than are necessary. Not only may the subroutines he selects be inappropriate, but it is also possible that the necessary subroutines are not available in the neophyte's repertoire of movement patterns. As a result, the learner is likely to fail to complete the executive program.

THE ACQUISITION OF SUBROUTINES

Since subroutines are extremely important in the total execution of a skill, the question arises, "How do people obtain effective subroutines?" Fitts and Posner (1967) suggested that *adults* learn new skills by re-

---

[4] K. S. Lashley, "The Problem of Social Order in Behavior," *Cerebral Mechanisms in Behavior,* ed. Lloyd A. Jeffress (New York: John Wiley & Sons, Inc., 1951), p. 115.

organizing or repatterning existing subroutines. If this is true, the necessity of establishing a repertoire of subroutines during childhood is obvious. Exposure to a wide variety of motor experiences in early years provide the adult with adequate subroutines to choose from when he is faced with a specific need or performance problem. John Anderson (1958), child growth and development authority, expressed the same point of view when he said, "The growing person builds a series of skills, one after another. . . . Patterns are built into his nervous system . . . an adult is a walking bundle of many skills which are ready to function even though only a few may be used on any particular occasion."[5]

Subroutines can be conceived of as "has-been" executive programs. Tying one's shoe lace was at one time an executive program. It then became a subroutine which runs off automatically. Subroutines are units or patterns of movements which have been relegated to a lower level of control.

Many individuals are hindered in performing a skilled movement simply because they do not have a large store of subroutines from which to draw, or the subroutines they do have are not effective. Basic skills are acquired early in life. J. B. Nash conducted an informal survey of recreational pursuits of graduate students. He found that the great majority first experienced their skills before they were twelve years old. Dr. Nash labeled the years between eight and twelve the "skill-learning years."

If an adult has a limited number of subroutines, he must compensate for this lack of subroutines. If he cannot compensate and cannot discipline himself to learn new subroutines, his chances of executing a skilled movement are extremely poor.

An example may be drawn from field hockey. One cannot be a skilled field hockey player if the subroutine of running is inefficient. If the individual runs fairly well but not very fast, he may be suited for a fullback's position. If his running skills are extremely poor, the individual should play goalie where the subroutine of running is not so crucial.

THE ORGANIZATION OF SUBROUTINES. The execution of a skilled act is serial in nature. Subroutines must be performed in a specific order in order to accomplish the executive program. The golf swing, for example, must be executed in a sequential order for a successful hit. The actions of the feet, hips, shoulders, arms, and wrists must follow one another. If this order of movements is changed, then the act generally appears awkward and the movement uncoordinated. The results are quite likely to be unsatisfactory. At best, the results will be less productive than if the sequential movement had been appropriately executed.

[5] J. Anderson, "Growth and Development Today: Implication for Physical Education," *Social Changes & Sports* (Washington, D.C.: AAHPER, 1958), p. 39.

Annett and Kay (1956) suggested that the skilled person has a knowledge of the sequence of events, which means he understands the serial organization of the task to be performed. The unskilled person lacks this knowledge.

The serial nature of a skilled movement can be discovered in various ways. Most movements have a preparatory phase, as well as an execution phase. Woodworth (1938) used the term "two-phase motor units" to emphasize the characteristic movements of preparation and execution. In the jump, for example, one crouches (preparatory) and extends (execution). The preparatory phase can also be thought of as the "preprogram" phase. In the case of the jump, the preparatory phase has certain mechanical advantages which insure better performance.

Just as there are certain *necessary* preparations which must be accomplished before the sequence of subroutines can be run off efficiently, some performers develop *unnecessary* preparatory movements. Despite the fact that some movements are unnecessary and may be detrimental, they can become vital preparatory actions to the run-off of the subroutine. A common example is the basketball player who cannot shoot until he has bounced the ball on the floor. A similar action exists among golfers who believe they must waggle the club before beginning the swing.

Preprogramming or preparation for the execution of a sport skill is important. Most physical educators are aware of the importance of "getting set" for action. Well-skilled players have learned the necessity of this phase. Unskilled players generally lack preprogramming. Learning and executing a preparatory phase may assist the execution phase which in turn aids the learner to organize the total act sequentially.

The idea of preprogramming also points out the necessity for a skilled act to be "started right." One has only to watch a skilled performer to notice the importance of starting the sequential run-off of the act correctly. The bowler, for example, always attempts to start the approach for his first ball in the same place. He tries to stand the same distance from the foul line in an effort to consistently use the same size steps in his approach. If he should take a large first step in his approach instead of his usual short half-step, the rest of the sequence is usually incorrect. He may, however, be successful if he compensates during the approach for the incorrect start. If the bowler does not compensate, the act is unskilled and lacking in effectiveness. The self-taught person often learns incorrect sequencing. Therefore, he generally has a more difficult time learning to compensate and requires a longer period of time to learn the skill correctly.

A good or correct executive plan can be helpful in determining the sequence of the subroutines. A beginner soon learns that in order to develop skill he must begin with a plan, and each subroutine must be sequenced in order to achieve the plan.

Individuals vary in their ability to organize subroutines. Some people are seemingly more capable of organizing materials in a sequential nature than others. Other individuals have difficulty arranging proper subroutines and need more reference to past experience or a different type of sensory input to aid them in organizing subroutines. Three sources may be involved in organizing subroutines to become operational. Learners may react favorably to (1) sensory input, (2) an executive plan, or (3) previous learning. The manner in which a skilled act is organized can be influenced by the immediate cues or sensory input, knowledge of the ideal or the goal of the act, and the availability of subroutines learned in the past or during previous experiences.

Some teachers of skills find it necessary to explain, give descriptive examples, and ask questions in order to aid the learner accomplish the operational organization of skills. In so doing immediate sensory cues are just as important as helping the learner to understand the total purpose or plan.

A skilled performer knows the sequence of events that is necessary to execute a certain movement. He also has an appreciation for *redundant information.* Redundancy implies repeatable events which are likely to follow one another. Research by Annett and Kay (1956) pointed out this awareness in skilled performers. The skilled performer also learns to ignore irrelevant information. An example of a redundant act helps to explain this quality. If you order "pie a la mode with ice cream" in a restaurant, you are using a redundant phrase. The "skilled" waitress has learned to ignore the redundant information. She interprets "pie a la mode" and ignores "ice cream." She may already be recording prices or giving you silverware . . . whatever comes next in the sequence of acts she performs. The skilled performer knows where to direct his attention and what information is irrelevant or superfluous, as well as what cues to attend to in order to obtain the necessary information to perform the task.

THE TEMPORAL PATTERNING OF SKILLS

Temporal patterning, another quality of a skilled act, is based on the capacity of the performer to *integrate* the sequential organization of the movement pattern. Temporal organization implies smoothness in connecting successive subroutines. It does not mean the speed at which a movement is executed or the total time taken to complete a movement.

The term *temporal* in this reference means the length of time or time interval between each successive subroutine.

The more expert or skilled the performer, the shorter and smoother the time in making the transition from one subroutine to another. The unskilled performer often moves in a jerky or mechanical way because he has not mastered the correct timing between each subroutine. As Bartlett (1958) pointed out an important quality of a skilled performance is that the performer appears to have "all the time in the world" to do what he wants. In other words a skilled performance looks effortless, primarily because of fluidity or flowing quality in running-off the total number of subroutines needed to perform the executive program.

PACING. The concept of pacing is involved in and greatly affects temporal patterning. *Pacing* as used in this context refers to the manner in which the total temporal pattern is regulated. In some cases, the performer has no control over the initiation of the movement pattern. External factors control the movement to a large extent. In a basketball game, for example, the player is constantly adjusting and timing his moves in relation to external stimuli (other players and the ball). In such cases movement patterns are *externally paced*. Similarly, a tennis player cannot necessarily control the rate of incoming information and, thus, is performing an externally paced task. The movement sequence of one's opponent and the opponent's placement of the ball determine the initiation of the next movement sequence.

In other sports the initiation of the movement is self-paced. The gymnastic performer generally executes a self-paced task. In a self-paced task, the performer can determine the rate of incoming information. Driving a car is a self-paced task because the driver can control the rate of on-coming information by setting his own acceleration speed. Action is both externally and internally paced when a person is driving in traffic.

Sport skills, such as skiing, can be termed self-paced tasks because the individual can initiate the movement and/or control to some extent the rate of incoming information. The skiier can slow down and take the turns at his own pace unless, of course, he loses his balance and hence, his control. Skiing on a crowded slope, however, changes the pacing modality.

In some sports, play occurs in a parallel manner. Players take turns alternating with opponents. In sports where parallel play occurs (golf, bowling, archery, etc.) external pacing plays an important role. For example, the golfer who deliberately slows down his pace to annoy his opponent is using the concept of pacing to "throw" his opponent's timing off. While some might label this as gamemanship rather than sportsmanship, nevertheless, this behavior does occur. The skilled performer becomes aware of this tactic and learns to concentrate on his own game. He can not let this type of tactic destroy his own sense of self-pacing.

This principle of pacing is also employed in team games whereby a team seeks to force the opponents to play at their pace. A coach may say, "We were able to make them play our game," if a team successfully sets the pace of the game.

ANTICIPATION. Another factor affecting temporal organization is anticipation. A skilled player "has all the time in the world" to execute his movement pattern because he has learned to anticipate.

According to Poulton (1952, 1957) there are two types of anticipation available to the performer, receptor anticipation, and perceptual anticipation. The two terms imply the origination of the information which aids the performer in anticipating necessary future movements.

Receptor anticipation is information which is received from the immediate environment and is external to the performer. It is a type of anticipatory feedback which aids the learner in programming his response. In tennis, the player who *sees* the opponent attempting a lob shot receives visual receptor information which helps him to anticipate the flight of the ball and, hence, enables him to adjust his next movement sequence and temporal patterning accordingly.

Perceptual anticipation involves information from internal sources and relies heavily on stored data. The tennis player who calls forth stored data on the past performance of his opponent and plans his strategy accordingly is using perceptual anticipation. Scouting reports supply coaches and players with information which will aid them in anticipating possible moves by their opponents. Perceptual anticipation relies mainly upon past memory and experiences.

Anticipation is extremely important for eventual successful temporal organization. Many times instructors of sport skills have utilized the concept of anticipation without realizing it. In tennis, the simple cue of "Get your racket back as you move into position" is a means of aiding sequential organization anticipation.

SUMMARY

Skills are organized in a hierarchical manner. In learning a skill the receptor-effector-feedback mechanisms are utilized. Information concerning the movement pattern arrives through the various receptors or input mechanisms. The central processing system perceptually organizes, translates, and stores this information relative to the *plan* or executive program which the learner wishes to accomplish. The effector or output carries out the executive program. Information relative to the successful execution of the movement is relayed back to the central processing system through the feedback mechanisms.

While executive programs provide overall direction and monitoring, subroutines are relatively automatic habits or fixed patterns of movement. Walking, for example, is a fixed sequence or subroutine of adults and is used to carry out certain executive plans. Executive plans determine the order and direction of subroutines. Early childhood experiences are important in establishing effective subroutines because subroutines were once executive plans which became habits. Children must learn to regulate their movements in order to develop an effective "storehouse" of subroutines for use in accomplishing skilled movements as adults. Adults learn skills by repatterning existing subroutines. If their subroutines are not effective, and the required ones are not available, they will have a difficult time accomplishing skilled tasks.

Skilled performers, as opposed to unskilled persons, have an appreciation for redundancy and attend to appropriate cues in the environment in organizing subroutines sequentially. Skills are organized serially through sensory input, the executive plan, and previous learning. All skills exhibit temporal characteristics, as well as sequential organization. The temporal patterning refers to the length of the interval between each successive subroutine. Temporal patterning is affected by the type of pacing (external or self-paced) involved in the task. Anticipation helps the performer to recognize redundant information. Both the receptors and central processing memory banks provide anticipatory information.

Fitts's definition of a skilled response involved the dynamic interplay of effector-receptor-feedback processes, as well as temporal and spatial organization. It is useful in gaining a complete operational understanding of the process involved in skill acquisition. Those who use this definition must examine how motor patterning occurs and must describe the qualities of a skilled act.

Research in physical education reflects the widespread use of descriptive definitions by physical educators, while the work of human performance theorists is more concerned with operational characteristics involved in skill learning. Both definitions must be considered in teaching physical education. However, the operational definition appears to be more helpful in the realm of the dynamics of skill acquisition.

CHAPTER FIVE

THE STAGES
OF LEARNING
A SKILL

Chapter 4 dealt with the qualities of a skilled act, including the hierarchical organization and sequential and temporal patterning, as well as the concepts related to executive plans, subroutines, and anticipation. Several questions arise from this discussion. How does man acquire the qualities of a skilled act? What capabilities must the various mechanisms (sensory, perceptual, and effector) have for the execution of a skill? What process or phases does man go through when learning a skill? When is sequencing important? When is the executive plan communicated to the learner? At what stage do executive plans become habits? When is temporal patterning important?

Fitts (1965) theorized that skill learning or the process of learning a skill can be studied by dividing the process into three phases. He labeled these phases (1) the cognitive phase, (2) the fixation phase, and (3) the autonomous phase. These three phases were determined from information obtained from an unpublished study conducted by Alfred Smode. Interviews were conducted with physical education teachers and coaches. Among the questions asked the educators were: What is the most difficult thing for beginners, intermediates, and advanced players to learn in a sport? How do you teach strategy? How long must a beginner practice before he knows a skill?

The interview study, which gave Fitts the information on which to base his phases of skill learning, indicated that there are four areas which receive particular emphasis in teaching. These areas are the cognitive aspects of learning, perceptual aspects, coordination, and tension-relaxation. Learning a skill involves forming an executive plan, as well as directing attention to selected stimuli, discriminating among cues in the environment, and continually processing feedback information.

Utilizing the work done by Fitts, the stages of learning a skill are enlarged in this chapter which includes discussion of (1) plan formation, (2) the practice session, and (3) the execution phase. Each of these phases is examined by determining what is to be learned, as well as looking at man's capacities for processing and handling information available during each phase.

PHASE I: PLAN FORMATION

Fitts (1965) termed the first phase of learning a skill the "cognitive phase." In this initial phase the learner must understand what the task or skill calls for; that is, the nature of the task and its objective or purpose. The learner must formulate an *executive plan,* and if he has acquired adequate verbal concepts, he may intellectualize the skill to some extent in Phase I.

During the formation of the executive plan, while he is acquiring a broad picture of the objective of the skill, the learner must also understand the *sequence* of the components of the movement. What is learned, then, during Phase I, is the serial or sequential organization of the task.

Demonstrations are commonly used to help the learner understand the objective or the purpose of the skill, as well as the sequential organization of subroutines. In addition to demonstrations, the teacher generally describes the act, also. Movies may be used to further aid the student in understanding what he needs to learn. Thus, the teacher uses auditory, visual, and perceptual modes during this first phase in order to help the learner accomplish the executive plan. In other words, the *receptor* and *perceptual* mechanisms are heavily utilized during the initial stages of skill learning.

In using these aids, the teacher must be aware of the functioning capacities of the receptor mechanisms. What are they capable of doing? How many should be involved? Some persons have suggested that every type of receptor organ available should be used to communicate the executive plan to the learner. The learner should see the movement, hear the verbal directions, and feel the movement. The answer as to how many receptor organs should be involved lies not in the *number* available, but in the capacity and limitations of the human receptor system. Channel capacity was discussed earlier (see Chapter 3), however, there are other human capacities and limitations to be considered.

MAN'S RECEPTOR CAPACITIES AND LIMITATIONS

The principles learned from experiments in the area of signal detection and recognition are applicable to understanding man's receptor capacities and limitations. One such principle involves the relationship of the *intensity* of the stimulus to the background. If the stimulus stands out, or is in deep contrast to the background, it is more likely to be detected. This implies that if people are to attend to a certain stimulus, there must be a contrast between the stimulus and the background. The surrounding context becomes extremely important.

Perhaps an example will help to explain what the principle regarding signal detection implies. A beginner in tennis may have trouble seeing a white tennis ball during a demonstration or during his own attempt to hit the ball because the white tennis ball blends in with the grey cement. Because the stimulus blends in with the background, the solution to the problem may be to intensify the relationship of the stimulus to the background. The use of red tennis balls against the grey cement background might aid the learner in attending to the stimulus. The new artificial surfaces for tennis courts that are colored green or red may have unexpected advantages for beginners. In the same manner "polar club golfers," who play golf in the winter, find it necessary to paint the golf balls red or orange in order to distinguish the golf ball from the snow.

SENSORY ACUITY. The effectiveness of sensory organs must be considered also. Sensory capacities may enhance or limit man's receptor abilities. Limited ability in depth perception, peripheral vision, visual acuity, and auditory functioning can greatly reduce man's ability to learn a skill.

Sensory acuity in this context refers to the physiological functioning of the various sensory organs. No matter how long or how often man practices, sensory acuity cannot be improved. Continual practice at viewing an object will not improve visual acuity. Vision must be corrected by artificial aids, such as eye glasses, which change the light refraction on the retina.

Although sensory acuity cannot be improved through practice, certain sense organs are more useful for detecting stimuli than others. For example, the most efficient types of warning devices make use of auditory modes as opposed to visual modes because audition is not directional. Likewise, a novel or unusual presentation of stimuli will be more easily detected than common or everyday occurrences. A blinking light on the dash board of a car will more likely attract attention than a steady light.

Loud noises will draw attention. Detection may also be improved through the use of rewards. Thus, praising one for noticing a certain stimulus affects detection.

SPECIFICITY OF DETECTION. The ability to detect certain stimuli is not transferable to detecting other stimuli. During World War II the question arose, would baseball umpires who have learned to detect and discriminate between pitched balls and strikes make good aircraft detectors? To answer this question it had to be determined whether or not the principle of detection is specific or general. The ability to detect balls and strikes is a highly specific task and it was found that the ability is not transferable to other discrimination tasks. Simply because a person has learned to detect a stimulus in one task does not mean that he will be able to detect stimuli in other tasks. Learning each new task must begin with detecting the stimulus in relationship to the background.

THE DOCTRINE OF PRIOR ENTRY. Man is limited in his capacity to attend to stimuli coming simultaneously from more than one sensory source. If signals come to both the ear and eye at the same time man will process or attend to the signals in serial order. We have noted that man operates as a single channel system (see page 35, Chapter 3). In dealing with signals arriving simultaneously, he has two alternatives. They can be disregarded or filtered out, or they can be "held" in short term sensory storage before being processed. The single channel hypothesis supports the idea that man has the ability to filter information.

Have you ever listened to a tape recording made in a crowded, noisy room? The sounds are very garbled because the tape recorder does not filter out any of the sounds. Every sound is recorded. Likewise, the person who uses a hearing aid for the first time finds it very annoying until he learns to filter out some of the "noise." Man can and does filter out irrelevant information. He does not actually process all available stimulus information. As will be seen later, this *selective attention* to certain stimulus events is extremely important in learning skills.

We have seen that man appears to possess some type of short term sensory storage system. Thus, a signal can be "held" for a few seconds and can wait its turn to be processed. The ability of man to hold a signal in short term storage is related to his ability to divide his attention between two sensory inputs. The term for this division of time is *time sharing*.

The question of time sharing was studied by Bahrick, Noble, and Fitts (1954). In their study two groups of subjects learned the simple skill of responding to lights by pushing certain keys. One group responded to lights which came on at *regular* intervals; the second group responded to lights which came on at *random* intervals. The task of pushing certain keys when the lights appeared was labeled the primary task. As a secondary task, both groups worked simple arithmetic problems while practicing responding to the lights.

The criterion test was observing which group would score higher on the secondary task. The results showed that the group that responded to regular light occurrences had the better scores on the arithmetic problems. The explanation of their success was that the primary task had become automatic, leaving the central processing system free to deal with such other signals as solving arithmetic problems. The group that responded to lights that came on at random intervals was forced to *time share* between the two tasks. Neither the primary nor secondary task became automatic. Thus the time required to process the sensory information was greater.

VIGILANCE DETECTION. Vigilance detection involves those tasks in which the person is required to respond only when certain predetermined events occur. Man's ability to perform vigilance type tasks depends on his monitoring capacity.

An official who referees a ball game performs a vigilance task. He must detect and identify rule infractions when they occur. If there were only one rule infraction to identify, the task would be much simpler than where there are many different types of rule infractions. Wherever or whenever there are numerous stimuli, the task is more difficult.

Man's monitoring capacity is dependent not only upon the number of stimuli sources available but upon the temporal rate of incoming information and spatial uncertainty of the stimuli as well. Man's effectiveness in monitoring depends upon his memory capacity which plays a part in his ability to compare an incoming stimulus with a standard. Generally speaking, man can recognize from five to ten stimuli along a single dimension. Judging a performance of a skilled movement is a type of vigilance task in which the number of stimulus inputs is important. Physical education teachers are constantly evaluating movement performance in order to give corrective measures.

Since man is limited in the amount of sensory information he can attend to during a given span of time, the rate of incoming information plays a vital role in man's effectiveness. If events occur slowly, then man can recognize and process sensory input. The rapidity with which most skills are completed precludes the necessity of the teacher to use additional aids by which to process sensory information. Check lists are one such method. Video-tape replay is another valuable method for aiding man to adjust the temporal rate of sensory information.

MAN'S PERCEPTUAL CAPACITIES AND LIMITATIONS

It is difficult to separate man's sensory capacities from his perceptual processes. What input man actually processes is highly dependent upon the perceptual mechanism. All skills involve the presentation of stimuli from the environment, and the resulting response to stimuli is possible because of processing done by the perceptual mechanism.

Perception, broadly defined, is the interpretation of sensory information. Man is constantly bombarded with stimuli. There are so many from so many sources man cannot and does not perceive all the various stimuli coming from all of the various receptors. Man must select certain stimuli from among all the possibilities.

The *process* of perception involves a series of coding operations. For example, when we see something, light waves are reflected by an object. This energy of light strikes the eyes causing chemical changes in the retina. These changes activate neurons, and nerve impulses travel to the brain. A chain of nerve impulses constantly passes between the eye and the brain. At the end of this stream of impulses, the perceptual process occurs. This should not be interpreted as implying that perception has a discrete beginning and ending; rather perception is an "ongoing" process.

Once the impulses reach the central processing system a series of different types of classifications of information takes place. Retrieval of stored data and codification of information completes the process. When one sees a four-legged animal, the impulses which travel to the brain are coded and the storage system of animals is checked until we recognize the animal as a dog.

Individuals perceive differently. As Leibowitz (1965) pointed out, individuals can honestly give different reports of the same objective scene. Realizing this fact aids us greatly in understanding man's limitations in learning skills. When a student says he cannot "see" or "understand" what he is to do in a movement pattern sequence, it is quite obvious that he is in fact "seeing" something different from what the instructor wants him to see. Several students may see a demonstration and have several different perceptions of what they are to do. The teacher may believe he is showing one thing and the students see something else. For example, the teacher may think he is demonstrating how to shoot a basket. The student may see only whether or not the basket is made.

Figure 4 presents several different but familiar sayings. Look at each of the sayings. Do you notice anything in particular about the phrases? As an experiment, reproduce these familiar sayings on a sheet

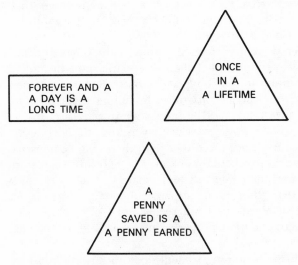

FIG. 4.   An Exercise in Visual Perception

of paper and ask several people to tell you whether they notice anything unusual about them.[1]

In the illustration used in Figure 4, most people are familiar with the phrases and at first do not notice the double letters. Further prodding tells them to process the information differently. When pressed, they may reprocess the information and perceive the double letter.

ATTENTION. Attention is the descriptive term used to explain which stimulus subsets are processed from a total stimulus field. As previously mentioned, man attends to different things. What he selects is not determined by the sense organs but is related to the perceptual process. Attention is the result of motivation, past experiences, and directions. Attention to something is a result of learning.

An individual is also aided in identifying or attending to certain stimuli by directions, instructions, or "set." If a student is instructed to "look for" a certain stimulus subset, then attention will be more likely directed towards that stimulus subset. After all, if one were given instructions to find the needle in the haystack, attention would be more likely focused on hunting for the needle. Man's receptor capacities may hinder him in finding the needle, but directions at least help him understand what it is he is trying to attend to.

The average gymnasium has a tremendous amount of stimuli bom-

[1] Generally you will find that people do not "perceive" the double letters.

barding the average beginning student. It is no wonder that students do not understand what they are to do when there are so many interesting things to perceive in the gym. Since man cannot attend to all stimuli, he will be selective in directing his attention.

Motivation or interest greatly affects attention. Many times students are motivated to attend to stimuli other than those important in understanding skill. For example, in watching a demonstration the teacher generally attempts to direct students' attention by telling them what to look for. The teacher may or may not be successful. In one case, where an attractively dressed woman golfer was demonstrating, the girls were looking at the matched outfit she wore rather than the swing demonstration. While auditory cues as to where to look may be helpful to some, in this instance the girls were motivated to look somewhere else. It must also be acknowledged that students are capable of looking intently at the teacher and/or the demonstration but seeing none of it. They appear to be directing their attention properly, but in reality are paying no attention at all.

In learning a skill, the beginning student does not always know to what he is to pay attention. Some beginners will not be able to see a movement pattern; for them, auditory stimuli through verbal description may be helpful. Others may have to experiment with the pattern for themselves and receive internal information from the sequential pattern of the subroutines before they can be knowledgeable about it. Whereas there is danger in using many methods or too many sources of input at once because of the possibility of "overloading the channel," too limited an approach can prevent students from seeking comprehension through a variety of methods.

In the early stages of skill learning, the student is not able to discriminate between revelant and irrelevant information. If the teacher gives too much information on how to perform a certain skill, some of the information will be processed and some will be filtered out. If the student filters out too much relevant material, the teacher complains that students simply do not listen. The teacher who gives too much information or explains too much may so overload the channel that "noise" is produced. Noise, in this case, is irrelevant information which distracts the learner.

When a student is shown how to do something at the same time it is being explained, he may not process or perceive all the information available. The teacher must learn to select what cues he wants the learner to attend to and must make every effort to help students see what he wants them to see.

The value of films and movies in helping students focus their attention on essential information should be considered at this point. As a general rule, physical educators have relied heavily on the use of audio-visual aids in various stages of learning. Sport films should be evaluated prior to using them so that the teacher can select the best time to use a particular film. Films must be used at a time when they can truly be an aid to learning. A movie is not necessarily good because it shows movement or motion. A movie can be an overwhelming experience for the new learner if it provides too much information at one time—much more than the learner can process with his maximum rate of input and lack of past experience. Many introductory sports films have this kind of problem built into them.

It is not difficult to understand why loop films are popular as learning aids. The amount of information can be controlled; the rate of input can be restricted and the information can be repeated as long as the learner needs it. Furthermore, loops can be selected according to the needs of individual students. Of similar value, but serving different needs are video-tape devices, including instant replay. This type of device, however, is more appropriate for correction purposes and therefore, is more suitable for use in Phases II and III.

In order for visual-aid devices to be of value to the learner, they (1) must be appropriate to the stage of learning and (2) must be used at the most appropriate time within that stage. If these conditions are disregarded, such devices can be detrimental to learning. Furthermore, showing a film when it is available, rather than when it is needed, is mostly entertainment and a waste of learning time. More attention should be given to the development of visual aids that are based on the stages of learning, instead of to the preparation of materals that are usable in a wide variety of situations.

SUMMARY OF PHASE I

During Phase I of learning of a skill, the student must attempt to formulate an executive plan. He does this within the capacities and limitations of his receptor and perceptual mechanisms.

Demonstrations may serve a major purpose during this phase of learning by showing the sequential ordering of the subroutines, as well as giving information about the executive program, the total purpose or objective being sought. Demonstrations communicate to the learner just what he is to learn.

In order to determine the values and the limitations of demonstrations, it is necessary to understand how man discriminates, identifies, or attends to selected stimuli. The majority of demonstrators rely more heavily on visual input than anything else. Thus, visual perception is an extremely important phenomenon for the teacher to understand. Visual perception is the ability of the person to organize and interpret information received from the sense of sight. The eye is not like a camera which records everything in sight; it adjusts according to motive, directions, and previous experiences. Persons watching demonstrations perceive what they see in different ways. Furthermore, they perceive what they want to perceive.

Although it is essential during the initial stages of learning that the beginner understand the sequence of the movement subroutines, it is not necessary that he imitate the form of an expert. Instead, the beginner must formulate his own movement plan according to his ability to perform the subroutines. He must, however, master the *sequence* of the components involved if he is to execute the skill successfully. For example, the golfer must learn to integrate the succession of forces necessary for a skillful execution of a golf swing. Likewise, a swimmer must learn the successful integration of breathing, stroking, and kicking.

The term "form" is used to indicate good technique and proper mechanical use of the body. Good techniques and proper body mechanics help an individual to accomplish an executive program. If he merely imitates the expert, chances are very good that he will be unable to perfect his own subroutines and complete his own unique executive plan.

The first phase of learning a skill, understanding the executive program, can be completed sometimes in a few minutes, a few hours, or a few days. The length of time it takes to complete the executive program and the sequencing of subroutines will vary according to the task to be learned. The important point for the teacher to remember is that the objective during Phase I is to be sure the learner *understands* what he is to do. This does not mean that he can or must do it . . . because actual performance and practice take place in the next phase of learning.

PHASE II: PRACTICE

After the learner has received and understood the executive plan, he must practice in order to fix the performance sequence in the human system. Fitts (1965) termed the practice period the "fixation phase" of skill learning. The amount of practice needed will vary with the complexity of the activity and the capabilities and past experiences of the individual. It is during this second phase of learning that the learner must engage in meaningful practice with emphasis on the temporal patterning of subroutines.

The *temporal* qualities of a skill must be mastered during Phase II. The timing and delicate control needed to bring in each subroutine of the task at the appropriate time must be developed, although refining coordination at this time may be extremely difficult for the learner.

How good the performer wants to be, that is, what skill level he sets for himself, will determine how long and how hard he will need to practice. Persons of different age levels approach this phase differently. Children practice to see what they can do. They seem to have no specific aspirations but they are extremely curious and, therefore, easily challenged. They seem to love to practice. Adults, on the other hand, want results quickly and often seek to achieve without putting forth much effort. If a particular component of a task requires a great deal of practice, if results are too long in coming, or if evidence of success is unsatisfactory to them, adults are inclined to lose interest and momentum.

Man's receptor and perceptual mechanisms play as important a role during the practice phases of learning a skill as they did during the formation of the executive plan. How man detects and processes stimuli information is as important during this stage of learning as it was during the cognitive phase or initial stage of learning. Thus, the reader should keep in mind the knowledge previously presented concerning man's receptor and perceptual capacities and limitations while adding the following information to it.

RECEPTOR CUES DURING PRACTICE

During the practice phase of learning a skill, demonstrations play a different role than they did in Phase I. During the first phase, demonstrations helped the learner establish the sequence of the subroutines. Demonstrations used during Phase II of learning should aid the player in smoothing out his performance; that is, help him master the temporal patterning of the skilled movement. Timing the component subroutines and the interval between the subroutines is an extremely important characteristic to be developed durng this second phase of learning.

Auditory cues can help the learner become aware of formerly unnoticed cues. The "swish" of the racquet, or the "ping" of the ball hitting the "sweet spot" on the tennis racquet are examples of useful auditory cues which help the learner gain temporal patterning, as are the sounds of the golf club hitting the ball, the bat striking the baseball and the basketball rebounding from a hardwood floor.

Visual cues, which are used mainly in demonstrations of the sequence of the movement during the formation of the executive plan, demand that the eyes focus at a certain spot, and thus require the head to be in a certain position. Auditory cues, on the other hand, do not require directionality for processing. The student can listen and perform.

The golf swing is often taught by demonstrating the stance, body placement, grip, head position, etc. and having the student repeat each progression after watching the instructor. It is impossible for the student to "see" the demonstration and maintain proper position. Auditory cues or verbal directions can be extremely helpful because the learner doesn't have to look up or move out of proper position in order to process additional information.

Demonstrations during this phase may serve to point out errors. A demonstration by the instructor that compares the incorrect sequence to the correct one can sometimes help the learner to see where his error occurred. Often during this stage of learning, the learner has repeated the incorrect sequence so many times that awareness of it has diminished. Thus, demonstrations of the incorrect sequence may serve to focus attention on the undesired sequence and result in its correction.

SCHEDULES AND DISTRIBUTION OF PRACTICE

How long should practice session be? Should practices be distributed or massed? When should rest periods be introduced? These are the questions which must be answered during the planning of Phase II of the learning of a skill.

Ebbinghaus in the late 1800's demonstrated that distributed trials of practice produce greater efficiency in learning than mass trials. Wheeler and Perkins (1932) proposed that the question of the effectiveness of distribution of practice depends greatly upon the age and the maturation of the individual. It would also seem likely that the length of practice periods is dependent upon motivation or desire. Observations of children at play indicate that as long as motivation is present, children apparently can stay at tasks for extended periods of time.

Kientzle (1946) found that distribution of practice may affect performance rather than learning, and hence, once the inhibitory effects of fatigue have been dissipated, performance is enhanced by mass practices. The person who is in poor physical condition and puts forth a great deal of effort, for example, a beginner, may benefit more from short, frequent practice periods. If fatigue and boredom set in during the practice session, the spacing of practices apparently facilitates learning. The tendency to use incorrect subroutines during practice increases as the muscle groups begin to tire. Therefore, frequent rest periods are important if fatigue or boredom occurs.

There is apparently no single optimal schedule for the learning of all skills. Each skill or task must be analyzed, and practice periods must be planned according to the learner's capacity, limitations, motivation, and stage of learning. For example, tasks which require a high degree of accuracy or precision are learned more easily with frequent rest periods. This can be observed in airplane spotters whose effectiveness at the radar scope improves with frequent rest periods. Vigilance type tasks, such as gymnastic judging, refereeing a basketball game, or shooting a gun, may be acquired more easily with frequent rest periods.

WHOLE AND PART LEARNING

Distribution of practice cannot be discussed without referring to whole and part learning. When we divide a task into parts, we are distributing the practice session. The practice of each part is a shorter practice unit than the practice of the whole.

One difficulty encountered in studying the effectiveness of whole or part learning has been the problem of distinguishing between a whole and a part. For some persons, the definition of a whole depends on how the individual perceives the whole, i.e., the whole is the largest amount the individual can handle.

Annett and Kay (1956) pointed out that the determination of what is a part and what is a whole has not proceeded in a very logical way. According to them, the procedure used to "partition" tasks has in some cases been as illogical as a surgeon's dividing up the human organism into sections of equal length. They further suggested that the nomenclature *part* and *whole* has been very misleading. The use of the terms *executive program* and *subroutines* and the process of task analysis may resolve the question of whole and part learning more effectively. Task analysis is the identification of the important components or elements of the task being learned, based on the total task organization.

Naylor and Briggs (1961) recommended that methods of teaching motor skills depend on the relationship between the task complexity and the task organization. Task complexity deals with the level of difficulty the task assumes for the learner. Task organization is the process whereby each subroutine is introduced at the optimal time. The task organization can be determined by ascertaining the relationship of the subroutines in the task. Some sequences of subroutines needed to carry out an executive program are highly independent of one another and are not usually performed together. Other subroutines are highly interdependent and seemingly "go together" automatically.

Independent sequences must be practiced as a "whole" in order for the learner to fixate or learn the order of the subroutines. They are not subject to control by each other, therefore if the executive plan calls for these independent subroutines they must be practiced together.

Interdependent or mutually dependent subroutines are best learned by dividing the task and practicing parts. This is especially true if errors occurring in the subroutines can cause larger errors in the entire sequence. If the learner cannot effectively execute a subroutine which is vital to the success of the executive plan he will benefit from part practice on this particular subroutine. Dependent subroutines must also be practiced separately when the executive plan requires that they be performed independently.

A brief analysis of a sport task will help to explain task organization and the dependency of subroutines. The completed executive program of the crawl stroke in swimming involves the subroutines of arm movements, feet movements, and breathing. These are independent subroutines which must be practiced as a whole in order to learn the entire sequential pattern of the crawl stroke. If however, a person has not learned to perform one of the subroutines, i.e., the leg movements, then this subroutine must be practiced separately. The components within this subroutine are highly interdependent, and there is a synchrony between the successive leg movements. Therefore, the kicking action must be practiced with both legs. If the subroutine of kicking is not performed effectively (i.e., force of leg thrust "down" instead of "up"), then practicing the entire sequence of arms, legs, and breathing will not correct this error. Since the subroutine of kicking is largely automatic, conscious processing of information regarding the leg action will be necessary for eventual correction.

Task analysis is preferable to task fractionation. The analysis of a task involves an examination of the dependency of the various subroutines and a study of the components. Many times a task is complicated by separating it into parts. The hierarchical nature of the skill, as well as the temporal patterning, must be considered.

ONGOING PROCESSING AND FEEDBACK

The importance of feedback during the practice phase of learning cannot be overemphasized. Since feedback represents the dynamic interplay between input and output, it is continually present in the acquisition and execution of skilled movements. The topic of feedback as an on-going process in skilled behavior is more fully examined in Chapter 7.

If the learner knows the executive plan or objective of the skill, he will know when he has achieved the expected results. If, for example, in teaching the spike in volleyball, the teacher describes measurable criteria for a successful spike, the learner will know when a successful spike has been achieved. A golfer generally knows how well the ball has been hit by looking to see where the ball went. He knows if it went too far or not far enough and whether or not his direction was satisfactory. He also knows if the shot was sliced or hooked.

If the performance is not to his liking, the learner probably does not know where in the sequence of the movement pattern he erred. He may have an idea but he cannot be sure at what point in the performance he made the mistake that resulted in making less than satisfactory impact, direction, or whatever. Self-analysis is not only extremely difficult, but is often inaccurate. The teacher, therefore, must be able to give meaningful feedback to those students who did not get good results. As a general rule, it is more meaningful for the student to be told when or why the error occurred, i.e., what caused the error, and be given a clue for correcting the performance than to be told that the objective was not accomplished.

Meaningful practice with appropriate feedback is necessary during the practice or fixation phases of learning. Practice alone is not sufficient, practice with feedback is necessary. Consider a person's handwriting. After writing his name for years, has a person's penmanship improved? Probably not. In fact it may be worse than it was five or ten years earlier. Each time he signs his name he practices the process, but such repetition does not constitute meaningful practice with feedback.

FEEDBACK AND ERRORS. Some teachers try to prevent mistakes from occurring. They want students to practice only the correct movement pattern. They should remember that every performer makes some errors some time. The more skilled the performer, the less frequent his mistakes, or the more narrow the range within which the mistakes occur. Errors are necessary for learning. Errors provide feedback and are vital for eventual success. If error is defined as the difference between the desired output and the actual output, all feedback can be thought of as error information. During the practice phase the performer attempts to reduce the range of errors between the movement pattern desired and the movement pattern produced.

In order for teachers to provide students with useful feedback, they must develop a trained eye and an empathetic feeling for a movement pattern. That is, they need to know the correct sequence of movement, and the timing, speed, and application of force of the movement pattern in order to be able to provide meaningful feedback to their students. This is not to say that all teachers must be well skilled in the sport they are teaching. However, teachers must develop a discriminatory eye for detecting errors in movement patterns and one way to develop this ability is to have learned the task which the student is attempting to learn. The teacher who has not mastered the task must, at least, have made a valiant effort to learn and in so doing, have experienced the movement.

Another way in which the teacher can develop a trained eye that will aid in providing feedback to students is to study the biomechanics and techniques of the movement pattern. This method is extremely helpful in understanding the sequential nature of the sport movement. All movements, skilled and unskilled, involve qualities of space, time, and effort. Therefore, the temporal qualities of the movement must also be studied. Too often, it seems, physical education teachers are concerned with the way a movement looks rather than the temporal qualites of the movement.

SUMMARY OF PHASE II

The second phase of learning a skill consists of meaningful practice with appropriate feedback, and it accents the temporal patterning of the subroutines. During the initial stages of learning a skill, the beginner must concentrate on the serial organization. Temporal patterning and refinement of coordination occurs during the second stages of practice. Although the executive plan may be communicated to the learner in a short time, the fixation stage or practice phase of learning takes a longer period. It is during the practice phase of learning that the question of optimum practice periods appears to be most relevant. The answer to practice periods must be determined through task analysis, capacities of the learner, interest and desire, and fatigue. There is apparently no single optimal schedule for the learning of all tasks.

Feedback is probably the single most important factor during the practice sessions. During Phase II, the learner is mastering the temporal patterning of the subroutines, and depends on feedback to help him accomplish this.

PHASE III. AUTOMATIC EXECUTION

The third phase of learning a skill is characterized by an increase in the ease with which a task or skill is accomplished, and a decrease in the stress and anxiety of the performer. Fitts (1965) labeled this phase the *autonomic phase,* which implies that the learner is now able to perform the total executive program almost without conscious effort. The performer has achieved the sequence of the movement through meaningful practice, has reduced his range of errors, has perfected his temporal patterning, and now performs the total movement pattern automatically with fairly consistent results.

It is during this phase in learning that the sequence can be thought of as having been relegated to a lower center. The quality of hierarchical organization has been attained. This relegation to a lower center frees the central processing system, allowing it to deal with other components of the task.

When the movement pattern is largely automatic, the performer can concentrate on other factors involved in the sport. The basketball player, having learned to shoot, can concentrate on evading his guard in order to gain a better position from which to execute a shot. The bowler whose approach is automatic can concentrate on the dart for spot bowling instead of thinking about the four-step approach.

After the performer has reached the autonomic phase of learning, his performance periodically "slumps." Sometimes it is possible to overcome the problem with long hours of conscientious practice. For example, the bowler whose ball fails to come-up into the pocket effectively for strikes, may bowl it out by practicing for hours on a "home lane," i.e., a lane that is very familiar to him. In other cases, however, the trained eye may be necessary to determine the error and suggest a correction. The remark "He's a pro's pro," refers to the individual who is so good at analysis that even the pro's contact him for help. The batter who is in a slump may choose to watch movies of his performance. He needs to examine the details of his temporal organization for the movement pattern and process feedback in order to identify variations that may be the cause of the increase in his range of error. If he is successful, he may regain his automatically executed performance. Occasionally, one hears of a fan who, watching a video replay, spots a variation in the performance of a favorite player and provides the clue to the "slump."

CHANGING THE SEQUENTIAL ORGANIZATION

In the above examples, the lack of effective temporal patterning was probably the main cause of the "slump" in performance. Sometimes, however, a performer may want to change something in the sequential organization of the movement pattern. Changing one's grip in golf, the number of steps in the approach in bowling, or the type of release in bowling are examples in which the subroutines and/or the *sequential* order of subroutines are modified. Performers who change their sequential order of performing a certain skill may find the change very difficult. Individuals often become discouraged before they reach their previous level of performance, much less experience improvement.

A major change is one in which either the order of the subroutines is modified or a different subroutine is used. The teacher who wishes to suggest a major change for a student should consider the problem carefully. The matter should be considered from the student's point of view, as well as from the teacher's point of view. It is usually wise to discuss the matter with the student and mutually agree to the advisability of a change. Perhaps the student is satisfied with his present performance and does not have the desire to make the necessary effort to change. If the student does not wish to change, it would be bad judgment on the part of the teacher to insist on it. Insistence can bring about undesirable results, including such a thorough dislike of the sport that the person refuses to participate in it again. Such was the case of a tennis player whose teacher insisted she use an eastern forehand grip instead of the preferred and effective continental grip.

There are other important considerations. There may not be enough time in class for the learner to make adequate progress. If improvement in performance is considered in the grading procedure, the student is unlikely to want to jeopardize the quality of his performance. Perhaps the student has been using his present technique for many years. Since the average sports participant rarely reaches the final automatic stage of skill learning before he has practiced for several years, it is extremely difficult to change a movement pattern in a few weeks.

It is probably easier for the learner to make small adjustments or minor changes in a subroutine than to change the sequential arrangement. For example, a bowler could modify his hand position more easily than he could change from a three step approach to a four step approach. The former involves a minor change in a subroutine, while the latter involves a major change in sequential arrangement, as well as the addition of a subroutine.

A small change in a subroutine could add to the perfection of the temporal patterning. Using another example from bowling, if the performer shortens his first step (which is a minor change in a subroutine), it will affect the timing of the arm swing and foot pattern. Shortening the first step usually corrects a "late" release in which the ball is released before the foul line instead of after the foul line.

A similar analysis can be made in regard to the push-a-way in bowling. Increasing the distance of the push-a-way generally results in an increase in the length of the back swing, provided the length of the first step is increased slightly. Obviously, the total temporal patterning is affected.

When an individual has reached the automatic stage in his learning, only minor changes should be encouraged. Woe to the teacher who insists a major change must be made and then discovers the student is unable to achieve as high a level of performance as that held before the change.

It is also easier to make changes in the first part of the sequence than in the middle of the sequence. Thus, if a bowler has a hop in the middle of his approach instead of a full step, the teacher must look at the beginning of the sequence for a possible correction cue. In this case the performer has an extra subroutine in the total movement pattern. Although this might at first appear to be a sequential problem, it is, in fact, a temporal problem. The bowler has to use the extra subroutine because his inital temporal patterning is off.

A minor change in one subroutine, such as adjusting the push-away in the ball swing, may improve this bowler's performance. If he is pushing the ball up and away, that is, towards the ceiling, the extra long swing may delay his backswing. It may also cause him to drop the ball toward the floor and lower his shoulder, which, in turn, shortens the back swing and affects the timing between the feet and arm swing. He must "hop" in the middle of his approach because there isn't time for a full step—the hop enables everything to catch up. Thus, he literally delays the feet action in order for his arm to catch up. If he is told to push the ball toward the pins, rather than toward the ceiling, the bowler will actually be changing the temporal patterning of the movement. Changing the direction of the push-away at the beginning of the approach will correct the error in the middle of his sequence.

NEW STRATEGIES FOR OLD PATTERNS. When the performer reaches the execution phase of his learning, his executive plan has become nearly automatic. When skills or executive plans become automatic they may be regarded as habits. Minor changes in execution may improve performance. However, at this point in learning, it is generally better to add new strategies which use existing methods of execution rather than to suggest a major change in the technique.

Physical education instructors tend to be unaware of the above statement. Inevitably, high school and college instructors start to teach a skill by discussing and demonstrating the "proper" form to be used. Sequential organzation is stressed. If a student has developed poor subroutines (remember that subroutines were once executive plans that have become automatic), the teacher tries to change them. For example, many girls who reach college have ineffective throwing patterns. Yet, these throwing patterns, by this time, have most likely become automatic and established subroutines. It is so difficult to change these subroutines that most girls probably cannot be motivated to try to change.

Since the subroutines cannot in all probability be changed, other adjustment needs to be made. Perhaps the strategy used in the game or sport can be changed and other strategies stressed. In this way, the students can learn to use tactics appropriate to their particular subroutines.

It is, of course, important that the performer and the teacher set reasonable goals. Few persons can achieve the skills of professional players on TV. There is also a difference in reasonable objectives held for different age levels. It may be reasonable, for example, to set the objective of hitting the golf ball for the child, of hitting the ball to the green for the adult, and of hitting the ball close to the pin for the professional.

Not everyone in a physical education class has the desire to become an expert player. If a player wishes to learn volleyball in order to become a "backyard" volleyball player, then his goals should be accepted by the instructor. It is the instructor's responsibility to do everything possible to aid the student to attain his goal. The instructor may also do everything possible to encourage the student to set new and higher goals. If, however, the teacher holds goals which are different from those the students hold for themselves, there will be class conflict.

When we speak of individual differences in performance, we must also keep in mind individual differences in terms of available subroutines. Not everyone has efficient and effective subroutines. If the player wishes to become an expert, he will have to work hard to improve his subroutines. Players who have the desire but lack effective subroutines must compensate for lack of skill by improving their strategy. The skilled player who is also a skilled strategist, however, has the best advantage.

There is some question as to when, in the process of acquiring of skill, strategy should be introduced. Some physical educators believe students should be exposed to strategy after they have acquired skill. However, it seems more sound to contend that simple strategies are applicable to simple skills and complex strategies accompany complex skills. Thus, appropriate strategies for using a skill must be taught when the skill is taught.

THE USE OF VIDEO TAPES. Television and video tapes are being used with increasing frequency in physical education settings. Coaches have enthusiastically welcomed video tape procedures as a means of improving the individual skills of players in a variety of sports. Viewing himself on the monitor, a player can observe the errors in his technique and thus, become better equipped to correct them. During the formation of the executive plan the beginning learner does not know what to look for. In the later stages of practice the learner becomes more conversant and knowledgeable about the entire sequential and temporal pattern. Seeing films of past performances can help him understand and direct his development.

One of many factors which can influence the benefits derived from viewing one's own performance is self-concept. Although it has not been thoroughly explored, in theory, performers and coaches may see on the tape only what they *expect to see* according to their preconceived ideas. Viewers may be restricted by the self-concept or "set" they bring to the viewing situation.

A study conducted by the author (Robb and Teeple, 1969) investigated the problem of objectively viewing oneself on video tape. A questionnaire was used to determine each student's self-perception of the kinds of movements each performed in his bowling approach. It included several questions. Some examples are:

1. Is the first step of your approach shortest of all?
2. Are your steps in the bowling approach progressively faster?
3. Do you slide to complete the approach?

Each student was filmed, and the following day each viewed his approach in a video-tape replay. The students again filled out the same questionnaire after they had seen themselves on the video tape. The results indicated very little or no significant change in self-perception of the bowling approach. Even though it was obvious to the experimenters that the answers on the questionnaire did not always reflect the actual performance, the bowler maintained his original perception, even after observing his approach several times on video tape.

An instructor also rated each bowler during the actual bowling and after viewing the students on the video tape. His ratings changed after viewing the video tape. This suggested the use of video tape in establishing the reliability of teacher ratings and evaluations. Taping allows repeated examinations of the same movement, while "on-line" performance does not. Thus, if a recorded pattern is available for study, the instructor is more likely to determine more errors of movement with greater accuracy.

The fact that the students did not alter their views indicated that perhaps self-viewing may cause a psychological block for detecting one's own errors, or there is a lack of interest in viewing for errors in performance, or both. Perhaps the student is more concerned with such things as facial expression and number of pins knocked down or correct movements rather than analytical error of performance. If this is true, viewing with consultation may aid in directing performer's attention to error in movements.

SUMMARY OF PHASE III

After the learner has become aware of the executve plan in Phase I and has fixed the sequential order in his mind, he practices execution of the skill in Phase II. During this practice session he gains proficiency in the temporal patterning, and he completes Phase III when the total sequential pattern becomes automatic. We must remember, however, that learning proceeds over a very long period of time and seldom stops. Thus, the execution phase of skill learning requires the application of the additional skill components, strategy and concentration.

Even though the sequential pattern has become automatic and has been relegated to a lower center, some type of monitoring is always taking place. When a performer has fixed in his mind the sequential and temporal patterning of a movement, during the executive phase he cannot think about what he is doing. In fact, sometimes the best cue he can be given is, *"Stop* thinking!"* This is because most skills are run-off with such rapidity that the central processing system cannot process information during an ongoing performance. Yet, some type of monitoring must be in process because many times a performer can change his sequence (make minor adjustments automatically) in the middle of a skill execution.

Although the performer is cautioned not to think *during* a performance, he should be taught to think through his sequential and temporal movement pattern *before* he performs. Once he is ready to begin, he must concentrate on either getting started correctly, his point of aim, or his strategy. He cannot think about the total movement pattern.

If major changes are made during the execution phase of learning, a change in the sequential arrangement of the skill is involved. Major changes should be underaken *only* if the student and the teacher realize the difficulty involved in accomplishing the change and if the student desires to change his style or technique. Otherwise, the teacher's role is to suggest minor changes in a subroutine and to increase the student's knowledge of the use of the skill in the game by emphasizing strategy. Strategy can be extremely helpful to a player who needs to compensate for poor subroutines.

The fact that strategy was mentioned in Phase III does not imply that this is where strategy should be taught. On the contrary, strategy is for all phases and levels. Beginning strategy should be taught to those players who are in the early stages of learning to execute a skill. Likewise, intermediate strategy should be taught during the intermediate stages and advanced strategy should be taught to players who have more skillful subroutines.

SUMMARY

In this chapter man was viewed as a single channel information processing system. Learning a skilled movement involves utilization of the receptor and perceptual capacities and limitations. These mechanisms attend to and select for processing certain stimuli in the environment. Man is limited in the rate and number of sensory modes for processing information.

Input signals are transformed into effector action as one learns a skill. Since man's capacity to perform several tasks simultaneously is limited, he must time-share. Through learning, tasks are organized into larger units and various subroutines are relegated to lower centers.

The process of learning a skill was arbitrarily divided into three phases which are similar to Fitt's cognitive, fixation, and autonomous phases. Phase I involves the formation of the executive program and the learning of the sequence of subroutines required in the task. The learner is busy during this phase sorting out relevant and irrelevant cues to process. He is refining and reducing his sequential errors. In order to accomplish the sequential organization, man must decide which stimulus information to attend to and process.

Practice with appropriate feedback occurs during Phase II. The learner's capacities and limitations must be considered in determining practice sessions, and the task must be analyzed to determine subroutines or parts that must be practiced separately or together. If the task contains subroutines that are highly independent or involve a synchrony of action, it is best learned as a whole. If, however, the subroutines are interdependent, they should be practiced separately.

Feedback provides error information. Future modification of responses depends upon knowledge of errors. Teachers can serve as one source of feedback if they develop a discriminatory eye for detecting errors in sequential and/or temporal patterning.

There is a gradual phasing into the so-called automatic phase of learning. It takes many years of practice to actually perfect a sequential movement pattern and learning continues over a long period of time. As various executive plans become automatic, the central processing system is freed to deal with areas of strategy and more advanced techniques. It is important to teach the appropriate strategies for the various levels of performance. In many cases strategy can be used to overcome poor or inefficient subroutines.

Man receives information and makes decisions which are translated into observable actions. The information presented in this chapter offers some insight into the complexities involved in this process of learning and/or acquiring skill.

CHAPTER SIX

FACTORS
AFFECTING
SKILL ACQUISITION

Chapter 5 discussed factors related to specific stages of learning a skill; this chapter will discuss factors which are important during all phases of skill learning. The study of skill acquisition is concerned not only with understanding "how" a skill is performed, but also in understanding "why" certain behavior occurs. Why are some performances outstanding and others mediocre? Why do people strive for excellency? Why do some people "remember" the sequential and temporal patterning of a skilled movement and others forget it? When should transfer of movement patterns be utilized in the learning situation?

The answers to these questions are examined under the topics of retention, transfer, and motivation. These topics are discussed in relationship to specific problems encountered in motor skill acquisition. Only a brief theoretical overview of each concept is presented here, but the reader is urged to supplement his knowledge of retention, transfer, and motivation with outside reading.

Also included in this chapter is a discussion of reaction and movement time. Man's ability to react and/or move and the understanding of these two factors are of extreme importance. Many sports call for quick decisions or reactions as well as speed.

RETENTION

Retention or memory is measured in the laboratory using any one of three different methods: (1) *recall* (2) *recognition,* and (3) *relearning.*

Recall requires a person to remember what he has learned previously. Essay tests, for example, require the use of recall. Recognition involves discrimination of several stimuli. Thus, a multiple choice examination is a recognition test. Relearning involves asking a subject to learn something, say, a poem or list of nonsense syllables. Then, after a rest period, he is asked to relearn the initial material. The time taken to relearn the material is the measure of retention. Recall and recognition tests result in a measure of the *amount* of material reproduced after a rest period whereas relearning requires the subject to "relearn" the entire material and thus is a measure of time.

Several theories attempt to explain how people retain information. The theoretical explanations regarding retention can be grouped into three categories: (1) interference theory, (2) memory trace theory, and (3) repression theory.

The interference theory is based on the assumption that forgetting occurs because the stimulus fails to maintain a relationship with a response. If substitute responses are associated with the original stimulus, then forgetting occurs. According to advocates of interference theory, the activity that occurs during the interval between learning and recall is of importance in the explanation of forgetting. Thus, if the central processing system engages in some other activity during the interval, the material is less likely to be remembered. The reason for this may be that interjecting another activity in the interval between learning and recall may prevent the person from rehearsing the material to be learned. Retention can be seriously altered if the material introduced in the interval is similar to the material to be retained.

Two types of interference have been identified or labelled to describe interference in retention due to interpolated learning. The term *retroactive inhibition* describes the situation in which a person who learns task A and then task B has difficulty recalling task A. Task B was interpolated between the interval of learning and recall and interfered with retention of task A. The more similar task B is to task A, the greater the interference likely to occur. Thus, if a person counts backwards after learning a group of numbers, then recalling the original numbers will be a difficult task because of the similarity of the interpolated activity which interfered with retention of the original material.

If task B is the task to be recalled, and retention is difficult because of previous learning of task A, then the term *proactive inhibition* is used. In both cases, some type of interference has caused the material to be forgotten.

The memory trace theory of retention suggests that each repetition of a performance wears a deeper neural pathway. The less frequently the pathway is used, or the greater the interval of time between recall of the response, the more simplified or superficial the traces between the stimulus and response become. Thus, forgetting is the result of nonuse.

The repression theory explains retention as the result of the emotional content associated with the material to be retained. We remember pleasant experiences and forget anxiety-provoking ones. The anxiety-provoking events are repressed or forced into the subconscious. They are still in the memory storage system, but they have been repressed and are not easily recalled. Since, these events are still in the storage system, the permanent memory hypothesis has been proposed. Although difficult to test experimentally, empirical evidence suggests that man recalls long past events which apparently have been stored somewhere. A certain cue or association causes these events to be recalled.

RETENTION OF MOTOR SKILLS

Although some studies have maintained that motor skills are more easily retained than verbal material, it does not seem valid to reason that material was retained mainly because it was motor in nature. Instead, it seems more likely that materials are recalled because of task organization or the meaningful patterning of responses.

There seems to be a relationship between retention and task integration or organization. This relationship is indicated by the previously discussed fact that a performer's level of proficiency greatly influences his retention. As we recall, sequential and temporal patterning must be learned in skill acquisition. This patterning can be thought of as the task organization. Reaching a high level of proficiency implies that the task has been highly organized both temporally and spatially. Skills that are highly retained are those in which a high degree of sequential and temporal patterning, or proficiency, has been achieved.

There is some indication that the sequence of the various subroutines in a movement pattern is more easily retained than the temporal patterning. For example, the performer who attempts a spike in volleyball following a period without practice usually retains the sequence of the total movement pattern but finds his "timing is off." Likewise after many years of not practicing, the person who learned to ride a bicycle in his youth can generally ride one, as an adult, but his initial attempt is characteristically unstable or wobbly. Perhaps what he has forgotten is the temporal patterning. Timing or the length of the intervals between successive subroutines is an extremely difficult component to learn. Thus the temporal patterning may be forgotten because it is not firmly "fixed" in the storage system.

If true, this theory should be considered in the organization of teaching units. It implies that the student who is reviewing a previously acquired skill needs to work on his temporal patterning since it is un-likely that he has forgotten the sequential organization of the skill. Thus, to begin a teaching unit with a review of sequential organization may not effectively aid the learner in regaining his temporal patterning.

TRANSFER OF LEARNING

The ability to apply previous learning acquired from one situation to a second situation is called transfer of learning. If there was no trans-fer of learning, man would be extremely hindered in acquiring knowl-edge and skill.

Theories of how transfer takes place have ranged from the formal discipline theory to the identical elements proposal to the generalization viewpoint. The formal discipline theory, which has been virtually dis-counted, stated that training mental faculties through the use of certain formal subject matter facilitated transfer. Thus, studying mathematics improved one's reasoning ability, studying science aided judgment and memory, and studying literature nurtured imagination and creativity. Through the use of formal subjects man was better able to train and discipline his mental faculties. This theory was disproven largely on the grounds that no subject has a prior claim in the training of certain faculties.

Thorndike, one of the leading proponents of the identical elements theory, believed that transfer takes place when identical elements exist. Those elements which are similar or identical to other elements in a learning situation will positively aid the learner, while dissimilar ele-ments will hinder the transfer of learning.

Gestalt theorists emphasized that transfer occurs through insight into the "whole" of a perceived situation. One learns general patterns, and cues which relate to previously formed patterns aid in transfer.

Many physical educators have emphasized the teaching of principles and generalizations in order to aid future acquisition of skill. Judd's study (1908) on learning to throw darts at underwater targets is one of the initial studies to support the teaching of generalizations and princi-ples. In this study one group of subjects was taught the principles of light refraction; another group practiced with no instruction on princi-ples. Although both groups at first did well as they practiced shooting darts at a target underwater, the group that had learned the principles of light refraction did considerably better after the target was moved to a new depth in the water.

Broer (1958) found that teaching sport activities would be more effective if preceded by instruction in general basic movements and principles of movements. However, Colville (1957) failed to find that understanding and applying principles facilitated initial learning of three motor skills. Although there is contradictory evidence, many teachers have continued to assume that the teaching of basic principles of movement will facilitate learning and understanding of skill acquisition and thus aid in *eventual* transfer. The Gestalt theorists support this belief. The importance of general principles and eventual success of this method depends upon the nature of the task, and the ability of the learner to understand and apply the principle. In other words, children may not learn by principles; they may learn by imitation. Adults, on the other hand, may be able to utilize principles during the cognitive phase of learning and will benefit from knowledge of principles.

Knowledge of principles of movement is extremely important and helpful to the teacher because it aids him in identifying which movements are fundamental in a certain movement pattern, as opposed to those movements which are personal idiosyncrasies of the performer. These principles also help the teacher to select the critical component to emphasize in teaching a task.

TRANSFER AND SKILL ACQUISITION

In order to better understand the role of transfer in the acquisition of skill, it may be helpful to determine the type of information used to aid transfer.

If we ask students to use an already learned movement pattern in the execution of a new skill, we are asking them to make an old response to a new stimulus or task. This is termed positive transfer. Learning to bat in softball transfers positively to learning to bat in baseball. The response is the same but the stimulus (ball) is different.

If on the other hand, we ask students to make either a different response from the response already learned or a new response to a specific stimulus, we are using the principles of negative transfer. Learning to bat left handed after previously learning to bat right handed is an example of negative transfer. Although it can be done, it is difficult because we are asking the performer to reorganize his pattern of movement.

Movement patterns that have become automatic are difficult to change. Under stress one will generally return to the old habit. Evidence of this can be seen in attempting to change the movement pattern of a basketball player who always bounces the ball before shooting. This subroutine can be eliminated through practice. However, under the stress of the game the player is apt to revert to his old habit. One explanation of difficulty in breaking habits is that the person is attempting to make a different response to the same stimulus. This is negative transfer.

One way in which transfer occurs more easily is if the instructor points out the similarities in the old and new responses by directing the learner's attention to certain cues. This is what is meant by "We must teach for transfer." When certain cues are pointed out to the learner, his *feedback loop* is enlarged. Certain information in memory storage is brought forth to aid the learner accomplish a new task. For example, pointing out the similarities in discrimination of visual cues used in ball tracking tasks, or similarities in strategy and anticipation can aid the learner to effectively transfer knowledge from one situation to another.

The reader will recall that adults learn new movement tasks by reorganizing previously learned subroutines. Information and direction will aid the learner to bring forth previously learned material. Specific cues given by the teacher can aid the learner recalling certain previously learned patterns which are similar to the new skill to be learned. Saying the movement pattern will "feel" like some other pattern may enlarge the learner's feedback information loop and thus aid him in the acquisition of skill.

MOTIVATION

Motivation theories are concerned with explaining "why" man behaves as he does. Motivation is not something a teacher can give to a student—that is not the teacher's job. A teacher does not have a "bag" of motivation to give to students. The teacher's role is to attempt to *understand* how people are motivated and to apply sound methods and techniques to enable the student to use and understand his own motivation.

Motivation is a prerequisite to any learning and plays an important role during the entire process of acquiring a skill. Human motivation is extremely complex. The very early studies of it dealt with instinct; today's theoretical explanations recognize the importance of learned or social needs as well as physiological needs.

GOAL SETTING AND LEVEL OF ASPIRATION

The German word *anspruchsniveau* was used in Lewin's original work and translated into English as *level of aspiration*. In its original use, the level of aspiration referred to one's subjective inner aim or expectations. Later experimentation attempted to quantify the term and referred to level of aspiration as *level of future performance in a task as specified by the individual.* It should be pointed out that there may be a difference between what one desires to do and what one will publicly announce he will do. Thus, level of aspiration as used in most experiments refers not necessarily to one's true aspiration, but to the quantitative indication an individual will make concerning his future performance in a task.

Success and failure deeply influence one's behavior. These terms are extremely complex—one cannot merely say that success produces the tendency to repeat the same experience. Just because one may have been successful in a class in performing a task does not mean he will want to repeat the same class, the same lessons, and the same drills. Likewise failure means different things to different people. A discus thrower who throws the discus 40 yards may feel successful. If, however, he throws the discus 50 yards the next day and 40 yards the day after that, he may feel that he failed on the third day, even though the same measurement caused a feeling of success on the first day.

It may be that no objective level of aspiration is set when one first attempts a task. Thus, he "gives it a try" with no level in mind and hence feels neither success nor failure.

The concepts of "what is success" and "what is failure" are linked to one's subjective interpretation of the two terms. Thus one's self-concept is involved. Self-concept is defined as how one perceives himself in relationship to the outside world. It is "I," "myself," and "me." One's self-concept may or may not be consistent with how the outside world perceives the person.

According to Syngg and Combs (1959), people form certain behavioral patterns in order to preserve and/or enhance their self-concept. These are: (1) mastery over something or somebody, (2) identification with successful people or institutions, and (3) the use of drugs or alcohol. When a person is successful in learning a skill, his self-concept is enhanced because of his mastery over the task.

Whether or not one's self-concept will be enhanced in a physical education class depends on the standard used to measure success. Using an expert's standard of skilled performance to measure a beginner's performance will result in a degradation of the self-concept. Physical educators have been guilty of setting demanding standards that are based on the performances of champions. Realistic standards are needed in order to evaluate beginners' progress. More precisely, we must identify standards that can be achieved by average performers after each series of lessons. Since failure is degrading to a student's self-concept, students who believe they are not successful (and therefore fail) will not likely want to continue to participate in a sport.

Progressive goal setting in physical education can be extremely helpful in applying the principle that success begets success. Instead of setting as the final task an expert's skilled performance, the teacher can help the student to success by establishing shorter goals at various levels, i.e., progressive goals.

An example can illustrate the idea of progressive goals. The first task for a learner in bowling could be to execute the approach and release so as to have the ball strike the 1-3 pocket. If the student can do this seven times out of ten, he is successfully progressing in learning the movement pattern. For the second task, the student should aim to hit the five pin by going through the 1-3 pocket. Each day's task can be progressively more difficult and demanding so that the skill learning increases with each new challenge.

Level of aspiration can be related to almost all forms of sports performance. The golfer who succeeds in breaking 100, will raise his level of aspiration and begin to work for a different, or in this case, a lower score. But if he always scores 99, he may not want to continue playing golf. Thus, enhancing one's self-concept is directly related to the level of aspiration and to one's need for achievement.

Often times a student is quite happy with a performance that the teacher believes is average or poor. The difference between the teacher's aspirations and those of the student can be a major cause of dissatisfaction and disappointment for both the teacher and the student, especially if neither understands what the other is seeking. The teacher must remember that the student's level of aspiration is what is important, rather than the teacher's level of aspiration.

This was evident to the author when, in teaching the game of squash to college girls, it was found that although some girls did not exhibit a single characteristic of the expert, they were, in fact, progressively improving. Upon watching one girl attempt to serve into the correct area, it was said, "Maybe squash isn't your game!" whereupon the girl turned and exclaimed, "But I love squash! This time I served the ball in one time out of twenty tries. And next time I'm going to get it in two times out of twenty!" Apparently, when we think in terms of motivation, level of aspiration, and self-concept, we must do more than give lip service to these theories. We must, in fact, aid the student by *listening* to him describe his goals.

Just as teachers sometimes fail to understand student aspirations which fall short of expertise, some coaches tend to overlook aspirations for expert performance in favor of winning performance. Unfortunately we often associate winning with excellence of performance; this is not necessarily a valid association. Games are won for reasons other than excellent performance. In the record book, however, the manner of winning is not recorded. The ultimate goal of every coach and every team should be excellence of performance. Coaches should be evaluated on their ability to help good performers become excellent performers. Unfortunately, too many coaches seek and achieve *personal* satisfaction from coaching winners. Many have little regard for the satisfactions achieved by individuals on the squad except as they reflect the coach's glory.

CULTURAL INFLUENCE AND MOTIVATION

Cultural anthropologists have stressed the importance of studying man's behavior in relation to his cultural milieu. Thus, society aids in determining what one's goals "should" be. The United States stresses achievement. We admire those who achieve success in school, in sports events, and in life.

According to Atkinson (1965) individuals vary in their need to achieve. He proposed the following formula to explain the components involved in need achievement:

$$T_s = M_s \times P_s \times I_s$$

(T_s) represents an individual's interest in a task and is a function of (M_s), the motive to achieve success, (P_s), the subjective probability of success, and (I_s), the incentive value. In Atkinson's formula, the motive to achieve success is a relatively stable disposition of the person. If this is true, then the *probability* of success and the *incentive* for success can be more easily manipulated than the motive to achieve.

The teacher can exert some control over the probability of success and the incentive value. The probability of success is largely dependent on the relative difficulty of the task. A task that is too easy or too difficult will not arouse or challenge the individual as much as one of intermediate difficulty. Likewise, a task that has no incentive value or is not highly prized will not motivate the person as much as one of intermediate value.

While some individuals have a stable disposition toward a motive to achieve success, other individuals have a motive to avoid failure (M_f). Atkinson's formula for the tendency to avoid failure is as follows:

$$T_{af} = M_f \times P_f \times I_f$$

The tendency to avoid failure (T_{af}) is a function of the probability of failure (P_f) and the incentive value (I_f). The level of difficulty of the task and the incentive value greatly affect the motivation of the individual. Failing at a very difficult task is not as embarrassing as failing at a very easy task. The person who wants to avoid failure may choose, if given a choice of tasks for which the incentive value is very high, a very easy task or a very difficult task. He expects to accomplish the very easy task, thus avoiding failure. If he chooses and fails the very difficult task it will not be as embarrassing to him as it would be to fail an intermediate level task. In the case of the very difficult task, he has a good excuse.

Previous successes and failures aid in determining the achievement motive. The child in physical education who continually fails in sports will not be likely to undertake sport tasks in the future. Continued grading by comparison will only cause poorer students to avoid failure. Avoidance of failure leads, in turn, to avoidance of activity. This is not to suggest that everyone be given high grades, because such a practice results in poor motivation. Making a task too easy does not provide an adequate challenge. Once again, an intermediate level of difficulty is needed.

Physical education students often have preconceived ideas of what the goal in a certain sport is. Watching bowling on TV makes the sport look easy but students should realize that years of practice and work have preceded the expert performance. Helping students to set realistic (or intermediate level) goals is the responsibility of the teacher.

ABILITY GROUPING

Matching students according to their ability is probably done more effectively in sport competition than in classroom situations. Great care is taken to ensure the equality of competitors through leagues, handicaps, and seeding. The probability for success is manipulated so that each player or team has approximately the same chance to win. The system is not infallible but it helps to equalize competition.

The theoretical argument for ability grouping is based on Atkinson's work. In a heterogeneous class, all levels of ability are represented. Success must seem impossible to the person of low ability or poor previous experience. The skillful student, however, is virtually assured of success. According to Atkinson's formula (see page 82), a very low or very high probability of success will arouse neither interest in achievement nor anxiety about failure. Therefore, only the students of average ability are likely to be motivated. This helps to explain why teachers tend to teach to the average—the average students are more interested.

Groups matched according to ability or previous experience become homogeneous and the probability of success is about 50 percent. Thus, previously low-ability students are now in a similar group where they have a chance for success, and high-ability groups are challenged because they, likewise, are in a similar group.

While the above argument is useful for equalizing competition, it does not always work for ability grouping of classes. Theoretically it should work; however, the class itself is not the only source of motivation. Thus, if a student is in a low-ability reading class, he, his parents, and his peers are aware of the term "low." Even if "low" is changed to "Level I," the students and their parents soon learn that Level I is lower than Level II in the reading groups. While the student may have success in the class, he may also be reminded at home that he is still in the "low" class. The fact that students are very much aware of low-ability and high-ability groupings causes an artificial situation. Once outside the homogeneous classroom, students, parents, and teachers identify success (and thus defeat) as the original purpose of grouping.

Progressive goal setting and realistic standards may partially solve the problems of motivation in physical education classes. For a beginner to achieve an expert's standard is impossible and thus degrading. In some cases, standards have been put in numerical form or in grading form rather than in terms of performance quality. When physical educators state class objectives, they should be specific as to what type of behavior must be exhibited in order to accomplish the objectives stated for the class. Bowling teachers need to help the bowler who has watched experts on television. Beginners should realize that this type of bowling occurs only after many years of practice.

TASK AND ENVIRONMENT DEMANDS

Of extreme importance in understanding why man behaves as he does is an examination of the demands of the task and/or the environment. Giving directions for a task not only conveys standards but also directs future behavior. Likewise, stress from the demands of the task affect performance and aid in explaining why certain behavior occurs.

Information input in the form of directions can cause stress which can either hinder or help the person attempting to perform the task. Increasing the *rate* of information will generally cause a person to work faster and faster until errors increase. Increasing the *amount* of information can also cause stress—the reader will recall that man's ability to process information is limited (see single channel hypothesis, p. 35). Thus, information overload causes man to either ignore certain information (possibly causing errors) or to stop work on the task completely. Man's behavior is greatly affected by the *type* of information he selects to process.

Removing all sensory input is as detrimental to behavior as over-loading the channel. Sensory deprivation studies have shown that under conditions totally void of sensory input, man becomes extremely agitated. Hallucinations may result. There is apparently an optimal amount of input that produces desirable results—people perform better under inter-mediate levels of input.

Directly related to information input is the question of speed and accuracy. Fitts (1966) conducted a study that pointed out how man handles directions concerning speed and accuracy. In his study, subjects in each of three groups performed a choice reaction time task. One group was instructed to be as accurate as possible on the reaction time task and was rewarded for accuracy. A second group was told to be as fast as possible and received extra points for making a fast response. A third group, the control group, was told to be as fast *and* as accurate as possi-ble. The results of this study showed that the speed group subjects were fastest, and the accuracy group made the fewest errors. The control group fell between the two other groups on both accuracy and error measure-ment. Man apparently has the ability to "trade off" speed and accuracy, and the result is a compromise between the fastest movement and the most accurate movement.

The results of the Fitts study are applicable to many of the require-ments of sport tasks. One of the more obvious examples of the trade-off function of man is seen in beginners learning to perform a tennis serve. In tennis, the beginner soon learns that to score he must be ac-curate. The "payoff" is getting the ball into the proper serving area. If he doesn't get the ball into the service area it doesn't matter how fast the ball traveled. A beginner's serve is generally slow and accurate be-cause the payoff favors accuracy.

Many times the teacher instructs the beginner in tennis to perform a fast serve. This is done, no doubt, because the teacher realizes that eventually the tennis player will need a fast serve that is difficult to re-turn. However, if the beginner doesn't see the immediate necessity of a fast serve, a conflict may arise between the teacher's objective and the student's realization of the payoff value.

Generally, the student will act as the control group subjects acted in Fitts' study. He will sacrifice some speed for accuracy and thus be assured of having the ball put into play, but will sacrifice some accuracy for speed in order to follow the teacher's instructions. When all else fails, he will serve fast when the teacher is looking and slowly when he is playing.

Fitts's results can be applied to any average tennis player. Since he has two attempts at a successful serve, the compromise will probably occur between the first and second attempt. The first attempt will be fast—if it is not successful, the second attempt will be slow and accurate.

The instructor who recognizes the "trade off" can attempt to remedy it in several ways. He may increase the size of the service area for the beginner, move the beginner closer to the net, or allow the beginner to compromise between speed and accuracy. If the instructor forces the student to stress speed, the result will be inaccurate serves. As the tennis player increased his skill and begins to play opponents who can easily return a soft serve, he will progress to a faster serve because the payoff value has changed. However, in the initial stages the beginner will inevitably sacrifice speed for accuracy.

REACTION AND MOVEMENT TIME

Man's ability to make a response is limited by the speed at which he can react to the stimuli. The time taken to initiate or begin a movement is called *reaction time*. It is that period of time taken to process the stimulus information. *Movement time* reflects the amount of time taken to complete the actual response after it has been initiated. Figure 5 presents a diagram showing the various terms of reaction time, movement time, and response time. As the figure shows, reaction time occurs just after stimulus awareness, and just before the start of a response. *Response time* is the total time taken to initiate and complete a response, and includes both reaction time and movement time.

REACTION TIME

Reaction time can be affected by several different variables—it is not necessarily a stable trait. Learning and anticipation can affect reaction time. Other variables are: (1) the probability or certainty of a stimulus occurring, (2) the presence or absence of a warning signal before the stimulus occurs, (3) the psychological refractory period, (4) the compatibility of the response to the stimulus, (5) the type of reaction time test, (6) the length of the neural impulse, and (7) set or directions.

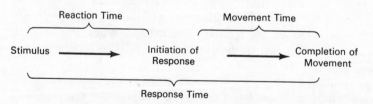

FIG. 5   REACTION TIME, MOVEMENT TIME, AND RESPONSE TIME

Reaction time is largely the result of central processing activity. Therefore, the more information a person must process, the longer the reaction time.

THE PROBABILITY OF STIMULUS OCCURRENCE. If a person knows when a stimulus will occur, reaction time may approach zero, due to anticipation. If a person cannot anticipate a stimulus, the reaction time will be longer than if the stimulus appears at regular intervals.

In sport skills, knowing the probability of an event occurring is extremely important for fast reaction time. For example, a guard in basketball knows that a forward always fakes to the right, and then attempts a shot at the basket. The guard's reaction time (i.e., defense against the forward) will be greatly improved by this knowledge. The guard will be able to time his response so that he can react at just the right moment to deflect the ball from its path to the basket.

Whether or not reaction time drills actually improve reaction time is largely dependent on the way the drill is organized. The drill must be structured so that the performer learns when an event will most likely occur. Successful drills must simulate the game situation. Blowing a whistle only tests a person's reaction time to the sound of a whistle. It will not necessarily transfer to a game situation unless the same probability of occurrence of the whistle is also in the game.

If a baseball batter knows that a pitcher always throws a certain type of ball after the first pitch, he can greatly improve his reaction time. Scouting reports can be of great help to determine the performance of the opposition. This knowledge and subsequent use of this knowledge to improve reaction time shows the importance of the central processing system and its affect on reaction time.

PRESENCE OR ABSENCE OF WARNING SIGNALS. A warning signal alerting a person to a stimulus affects reaction time, as well. In reaction time tests, the length of time between the warning signal and the stimulus is termed the *foreperiod.*

Starters in races generally try to be very consistent in the pauses between "on your mark" (a warning signal) and "go" (the stimulus signal). Any variance in the length of the foreperiod will cause false starts and present unequal chances for the performers.

An investigation of the effects of length of foreperiod on reaction time was conducted by Drazin (1961). In this experiment the foreperiod varied from two seconds to .125 seconds. The results indicated that the reaction time was slower for relatively short foreperiods. When the range of foreperiods exceeded five-tenths of a second, reaction time tended to decrease initially as a negatively accelerated function of foreperiod. Reaction time also depended upon the length of interval between the two presentations and reactions, as well as whether or not the stimuli were the same or different.

PSYCHOLOGICAL REFRACTORY PERIOD. Fitts and Posner (1967) have found that when the interval between reactions to two different stimuli is .5 seconds or shorter, the psychological refractory period limits the rate at which man can respond to successive stimuli.

The explanation of the psychological refractory period is that the delay is due to the processing time. Davis (1957) and Creamer (1963) presented evidence that delays in reaction time occur when one signal is visual and the other auditory, as well as when responses are with opposite hands. This indicates that delays are not entirely due to length of neural impulses but also to a limited capacity of the central processing system.

STIMULUS-RESPONSE COMPATIBILITY. The compatibility of the relationship between the stimulus and the response also affects a person's reaction time. Using a typewriter keyboard for response keys, a light panel arranged in a similar pattern will effect a faster reaction time than if the panel is not compatible with the response keys. This indicates that learning or training affects reaction time.

Stimulus-response compatibility is present in stereotype movements. Examples of stereotype movement are the way wall light switches operate and direction of hot and cold water faucets. If the response is altered so that it is not what we expect or what we are used to, then reaction time will be slower.

Most of our behavior in performing simple motor tasks is organized on a left to right basis. We read and write in this manner. We can hypothesize, then, that reaction time in turning dials will be faster in a left to right relationship than in a right to left one.

TYPES OF REACTION TIME TESTS. There are many ways to arrange a reaction time test. The two generally accepted classifications are simple reaction time and choice reaction time.

In a simple reaction time test (Type A), the subject is asked to react to a stimulus by making a specified response. There is one stimulus and one response. Pushing a button when a light comes on, or flicking a switch after a specified sound are examples of simple reaction time tests. A timing device records the delay between the occurrence of the stimulus and the initiation of the response.

Choice reaction time tests can be of two different types. In Type B, the subject is asked to respond to several stimuli. Reacting to lights displayed on a panel by pushing the appropriate response key is an example. The subject must learn the proper response for each stimulus.

A Type C test presents several stimuli but requires only one response. The subjects' task is to learn when to respond to a specified stimulus.

Figure 6 presents a diagram showing the various types of reaction time tests. Reaction time is affected by the type of reaction time test. The more choices a person has, the more information he must process, and hence the longer the reaction time. Type B, which has a possibility of several stimuli, each of which may or may not occur, and several responses, each of which may or may not be the appropriate response, will result in the slowest reaction time in comparison with the other types of tests. Type A, which has only one stimulus and one response, will result in the fastest reaction time. Type C test will result in a reaction time somewhere between Type A and Type B. Thus reaction time of one person will vary depending upon which of the three types of tests is used.

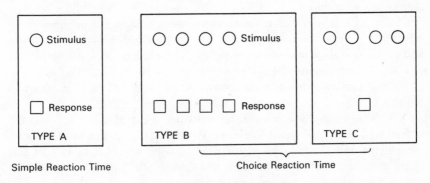

FIG. 6   TYPE A, B, AND C REACTION TIME TESTS

THE NEURAL IMPULSE. Although most delays in reaction time occur because of a central processing delay, individual differences in reaction time is also affected by the length of the neural pathways. Thus, a short person has a faster reaction time possibility than a tall person. In the 1850s, Helmholtz pointed out that the amount of time taken for the impulse to travel along the nerve affects reaction time. Helmholtz established the speed of a nerve impulse at 100 meters per second for the greater sensory and motor pathways. Since one meter equals 39.37 inches or 3.28 feet, impulses in the larger nerves travel at the rate of approximately 328 feet per second. Smaller nerves have a correspondingly slower rate of conduction (3 feet per second). The physiological process of conducting a nerve impulse also has an absolute refractory period during which no stimulus appears to be able to excite an impulse. This absolute refractory period lasts from .5 to 3 milliseconds.

SET OR DIRECTIONS. The directions given to subjects in experiments also affect reaction time. Directions refer to the amount of information a person is given about responding to a task. If a person is aware of what is to happen he can plan and modify his response. Telling a basketball player to watch for the fakes by concentrating on the midsection of the opponent aids him to anticipate a possible fake. If the midsection of an opponent moves, then the opponent will move in that direction. Similarly studying films of future opponents can aid the player to shorten his own reaction time because he "knows what to look for."

MOVEMENT TIME

Movement time is the lapse of time after the movement is initiated and until its completion. Movement time must be studied by separating it from reaction time.

Fitts (1954) found that movement time is related to the amount of information demanded, and to the particular conditions of amplitude and target size. If a movement requires precise accuracy at the termination of the movement, then movement time will be slower. The most important variable affecting movement time is the difficulty or accuracy required.

If little accuracy is involved, increasing the amplitude or distance moved will not be as greatly affected. If the distance is the same for two movements and accuracy is required in one movement, but not in the other then the movement requiring accuracy will be slower than the movement which does not require accuracy.

Relay racers in track events who must be accurate in passing the baton to the next racer may tend to slow down their final movement in order to be accurate in passing the baton. Since this is not desirable for an efficient racer, the alternative is to have the baton always in the same place so that the racer can anticipate and plan for the transfer of the baton. Randomness of baton placement will necessitate a slowing down of the runners.

SUMMARY

The topics of retention, transfer of learning, and motivation as they relate to skill learning were examined in the first part of this chapter. Various theories of retention were briefly discussed. Variables such as length of material, meaningfulness, interference activities, amount of overlearning, novelty, and level of proficiency reached during practice all affect retention.

Transfer of previous experiences to aid in the acquisition of a new skill is an important factor to consider in skill acquisition. Negative and positive transfer appear to be related to specific components of a skill or task rather than to a generalized pattern.

The topic of motivation was discussed briefly with particular emphasis on the level of aspiration, need achievement and ability grouping.

Effector action is seen in man's ability to react and move. Reaction time is the result of central processing activity and thus is an indicator of decision-making ability. Physical educators have not always made distinctions among the various types of reaction times and their methods of instruction have reflected this lack of knowledge.

Reaction time is the time taken to initiate a movement whereas movement time is the time taken to complete a movement. Variables that affect reaction time are different from those that affect movement time. Reaction time is the time taken to process information whereas movement time is the time taken to complete a movement. Accuracy will affect movement time but will not affect reaction time.

CHAPTER SEVEN

FEEDBACK
AND
SKILL LEARNING

Feedback is one of the most important concepts in learning. Wiener (1961) suggested that what control engineers referred to as feedback is an extremely important factor in the control of human movement and behavior. Bilodeau and Bilodeau (1961) agreed with Wiener in the importance of feedback, and emphasized that it is one of the strongest and most important variables controlling learning and human behavior.

The cybernetic approach to learning emphasizes that man operates as an information processing system. Information about the state of the environment is constantly being fed into the central processing system. The information is either stored or used to direct patterns of behavior. Information processing is an ongoing activity, and the state of the system output with respect to a plan or a goal (cybernetic jargon for what you are doing) is constantly being monitored within the human system. The monitoring system produces new input to the central processing system. Feedback can be that *new* information input, or it can be information about the consequence of a response that has just been performed.

Many textbooks use the terms feedback, reward, reinforcement, and knowledge of results interchangeably. However, with increasing research and understanding of feedback, it seems more appropriate to use terms that more fully distinguish the type, mode, and role of feedback, rather than using the term, feedback, to refer to any and all types of information.

DEFINITIONS OF FEEDBACK

Wiener (1961) defined feedback in the following way:

> . . . when we desire a motion to follow a given pattern the difference between this pattern and the actual performed motion is used as new input to cause the part regulated to move in such a way as to bring its motion closer to that given by the pattern (p. 6).[1]

Many psychologists working in the area of human performance agree with Wiener and think of feedback as providing error information. In other words, feedback provides the information with which to compare output to a reference or standard established by the experimenter, teacher, or learner. In order to correct future behavior a reference level or standard must be established, and the learner's output must be compared to this standard.

Bilodeau (1966) preferred to use the term *information feedback* rather than feedback. Her definition of information is similar to Wiener's. She stated that information feedback is the discrepancy between the goal and the obtained response, in other words, error information.

In the view of many persons, the term "knowledge of results" is synonymous with feedback. It is quite easy to understand why teachers, especially, would think of feedback as knowledge of results. After all, teachers are unable to provide much error information except after the performance when the knowledge of results can be determined. There are several different types of feedback. To be as accurate as possible, the terms feedback and information feedback are being used in skill-learning research to mean all kinds of feedback rather than just knowledge of results.

Smith and Smith (1966) used the term "dynamic sensory feedback" to describe the dynamic interplay of information and self-regulatory movement. It becomes more and more apparent that confusion concerning the use and misuse of feedback is due in part to the lack of a clear definition of the term. Therefore, for our discussion, feedback is information that arrives constantly during, and as the consequence of, one's own response, or that arrives as new information input from external sources. In both cases, feedback is used to compare present behavior to a reference response or movement pattern, i.e., a goal or standard.

1 Norbert Wiener, *Cybernetics* (Cambridge, Mass.: M.I.T. Press, 1961). Reprinted by permission.

THE ROLE OF FEEDBACK

Most experts agree that feedback can either motivate, reinforce, and/or regulate behavior. It regulates in that it provides moment-to-moment information relevant to the organization of the next response phase. It can be reinforcing in that information rewarding an acceptable performance increases the probability of repeating a similar performance. It is motivating in the sense that information stimulates the operator to try harder on subsequent trials.

ACTION AND LEARNING FEEDBACK

Miller (1953) used the terms action and learning feedback to describe the regulating and reinforcing roles of feedback. Action feedback is information regarding the changing state of an attempt to produce a certain response. Action feedback may not produce a permanent change in behavior. Learning feedback implies information which does cause a more or less permanent change in behavior.

Adams (1964) used the terms reinforcing and regulating feedback according to how each affected learning and performance. Regulating feedback, like action feedback, may affect performance but not learning, whereas reinforcing feedback or learning feedback may have profound effects on learning. Annett and Kay (1957) pointed out that the distinction between action (regulating) and learning (reinforcing) feedback is not always clear. The difficulty is that in some cases the feedback called action feedback is actually learning feedback.

Action and learning feedback are used in sports activities. For example, in bowling many performers use a wrist band. The wrist band serves as a reminder to the bowler to keep his wrist straight during the arm swing and the subsequent release of the bowling ball. Removal of the wrist band may allow the performer to "forget" and to bend his wrist. In this case, the performer received action feedback. If, after the removal of the wrist band, the performer could keep his wrist straight, the wrist band could have been the cause of a more or less permanent change, that is, "learning." This feedback should be termed learning or reinforcing feedback.

It should be noted that feedback is always present and is always regulating behavior. The terms *action* and *learning feedback* are appropriate for describing the temporary (action) or permanent (learning) effects of feedback.

MOTIVATING FEEDBACK

Feedback also motivates behavior. This motivating role is extremely complex because there is nothing intrinsically motivating about feedback. Feedback that motivates some persons may inhibit others. As a general rule, it is difficult for a teacher to know when feedback will inhibit or motivate behavior.

As discussed earlier, feedback can be thought of as error information. The term "error" may inhibit behavior if the learner's connotation of error is criticism. Since the teacher is a source of feedback, pointing out errors may actually inhibit rather than motivate the learner. It may be that a certain rapport between student and teacher must be established before error information can play a motivating role.

Pointing out errors in movement patterns can have the same connotation to the learner as punishment. Mowrer (1960) used the terms passive and active avoidance learning. Passive avoidance learning means the student learns to avoid making a response for which he will be punished. Punishment appears to work as a temporary inhibitor, and does not always produce a permanent weakening of the incorrect response. If the learner does interpret error correction as punishment, any change in behavior may be only temporary. The motivating effect may be temporary, also.

Active avoidance learning is far more promising than passive avoidance. Active avoidance learning involves learning to make a response in order to prevent the occurrence of some unpleasant event. Travers, Reid, and Von Wagenen (1964) urged caution in the use of adversive stimuli because of the fear and anxiety associated with punishment.

Smode (1958) found some indication that *additional* feedback information could prove useful in motivating performance on a task. A subject may attend to or be motivated by additional information or feedback that forces him to concentrate on a particular area of the task. Hence, he may increase his learning through an increase in motivation. (See augmented feedback later in this chapter.)

Ammons (1956) cited several studies that showed that the most common effect of feedback is to increase motivation. In general, information about one's performance affects one's incentive to do well. However, it is important to know what the learner is motivated to do when knowledge of performance is presented. Teachers need to be especially careful about what kinds of behavior they reward. For example, a grading system based on improvement rather than on the end result, may motivate students to do poorly in the beginning in order to show a high amount of improvement.

Performance information may cause some students to value the information rather than use the information to improve performance. Grades, for example, may motivate the student to "beat the system" or "take advantage of the system" rather than improve his own performance. Teachers must be alert to the kinds of things students are motivated to do as a result of the type of feedback given. Teachers must be extremely careful to use feedback as an incentive to improve actual performance.

FACTORS AFFECTING THE ROLE OF FEEDBACK

Other factors that affect the role of feedback are: (1) the stage of learning, (2) the arrival time of the feedback, and (3) the task to be learned. These factors are in addition to the learner's interpretation of feedback as a motivation.

STAGE OF LEARNING. Berlin (1959) studied the effects of different teaching methods during the early learning of motor skills. She found that following a general orientation to the task, the learning of selected skills by beginners was greatly fostered by actual uninterrupted practice. Demonstrations by skilled performers, visual aids, and verbal directions in combination with uninterrupted practices were also effective. Visual aids and verbal analyses by themselves ranked low in value as aids to learning. The results were interpreted to indicate that demonstrations play an important role in aiding students to gain insight into the objectives of the skill and to motivate the learners.

Uninterrupted practice is practice during which the only feedback is the result of the learner's own feelings and observations. The teacher does nothing, offers no directions or suggestions. Additional information is known as *augmented feedback*. It may take several forms and is extra information afforded the student while he is learning.

VonBuseck (1965) supported Berlin's findings when he found that during the early or beginning stages of learning, the subjects in his study did not benefit from augmented feedback. He suggested that subjects could not process additional feedback or information.

Analyzing the results of these studies in terms of feedback research, one can see that beginners were not aided by augmented feedback in the early stages of learning. This leads one to question the usual method of teaching skills in physical education. The teacher is always present and apparently feels the need to provide information or augmented feedback. Perhaps the students need a period of time or a period of uninterrupted practice in which they can sort out and utilize their internal feedback. Providing additional information or augmented feedback during the intermediate or later stages of learning may be more effective than during the beginning stages.

ARRIVAL TIME. At what moment should information be supplied to the student? Should one wait until the movement is over, or should information be supplied during the movement, that is, while the movement is being executed. The arrival time of information is identified as terminal or concurrent. If the information is "ongoing" and is provided during the execution for moment-to-moment regulation of behavior, it is referred to as *concurrent feedback. Terminal feedback* is a summary reference provided by the teacher or experimenter *after* a response pattern has been executed.

In sports performances, watching to see whether the ball goes into the basket or not is an example of receiving terminal feedback. In other words, after the performance has terminated, the information is available. Receiving a grade in a class is another type of terminal feedback.

Concurrent feedback is more difficult to arrange. Perhaps one of the most effective types of concurrent feedback has been termed "kinesthetic sense" by physical educators. One of the problems involved in relying on proprioceptors for feedback of an internal nature is in knowing how the set standard performance feels to the performer trying to learn it. For this reason, early studies of learning by physical educators based on kinesthesis produced controversial results. Learning to perform by the way the performance "feels" is difficult at best and especially so for a beginner. If, for example, in learning the golf swing, some type of device could be arranged so that at the top of the backswing one could "know" if he were overswinging (e.g., by feeling a pain), he would have immediate information during the action—concurrent feedback.

Depriving the learner of feedback is related to the arrival time of feedback. What happens in deprivation of feedback is that the experimenter is generally manipulating reference patterns rather than depriving the subject of feedback as such. The learner's performance deteriorates because of the lack of a precise standard by which to obtain error information rather than because of the removal of all feedback. It must be pointed out here that it is virtually impossible to design studies in which all feedback is eliminated. Internal or proprioceptive feedback is always present.

It is generally accepted that removal of terminal feedback (or any knowledge of the result of how one performed) causes a certain deterioration in performance. In this case the learner may have an adequate standard or reference pattern; however, he cannot compare performance except through internal feedback. If terminal feedback were provided through external modes, he would be aided in obtaining more information and thus performance would be enhanced.

One of the earliest studies done in this area was conducted by Judd (1905). Judd found that subjects who were not provided with knowledge of their results lost interest and became bored. Thus, no terminal information caused a decrease in motivation.

More recent studies have been concerned with the delay of feedback. Delayed feedback is related to the arrival time of feedback, also. Once again the type of feedback which is delayed is important. Delayed *terminal* feedback may not be detrimental to performance, while delayed *concurrent* feedback may be extremely detrimental. K. U. Smith has done extensive research in the area of delayed sensory (concurrent) feedback. Beginning with the effects of delayed audiotaped sensory feedback, and progressing to the use of computor-delayed types of sensory feedback, Smith has found that delayed sensory feedback is quite detrimental to performance.

In the studies concerned with delayed auditory feedback (Smith, Ansell, Koehler, and Servos, 1964), delayed eye movement-retinal feedback (Smith, 1970), and delayed feedback of movements of handwriting (Smith and Schappe, 1970), it was shown that delayed sensory feedback profoundly disrupts performance. Learning to adjust to delayed sensory feedback is an insurmountable problem for man. In fact, delayed sensory feedback is probably more detrimental to man's performance than the deprivation or total removal of feedback.

As an example of delayed auditory feedback, it is suggested the reader first imagine being unable to hear himself speak. Then imagine speaking in an echo tube in which the echo reverberates on the end of each word. Then imagine having the words come back several words late—one's thoughts are completely disrupted.

On the other hand, delayed *terminal* feedback or delayed information concerning a performance that has been completed may not be as detrimental. Teaching machines have been advocated because immediate knowledge of performance can be supplied to the learner. However, man has a memory and can no doubt "stand" delay of knowledge of performance. Certainly we know that while students are anxious to learn the results of an examination, it has not appeared to affect subsequent performances if the exams are not returned immediately. In fact, there is some evidence to support the fact that delay in receiving terminal feedback may improve retention (Brackbill, 1962, 1963, 1964).

The important distinction concerning the delay of feedback lies in whether or not the feedback is of a concurrent sensory nature or of a terminal type. Certainly concurrent sensory feedback, which is internal, is vital to ongoing performance and any delay in receiving this information will disrupt performance. One can imagine how difficult it would be to talk coherently if the sound of one's voice were delayed a few seconds. However, if the information delayed is of the terminal type, then performance will not be disrupted unless the learner becomes bored, disinterested, or frustrated.

Arrival time of feedback can further be described in relation to the use of a particular sensory mode. If feedback is eliminated from one sensory source, man quickly adapts to determine information from another source. Poulton (1952) found that subjects could respond for five seconds with their eyes shut after a short learning period on a type of tracking task. The elimination of vision had no appreciable effects upon performance in this brief period. Since the visual feedback loop was not providing information concerning performance, subjects were forced to find other modes of sensory input from which to obtain information, and may have relied on feedback from the memory storage banks.

Diehl and Seible (1962) conducted a typing study in which skilled typists were required to type under four different conditions: (1) normal speed typing; (2) normal but no sight of printed lines; (3) normal but the sound of the typewriter was masked; and (4) a combination of the last two. These conditions produced no appreciable differences in results as measured by speed and accuracy scores. Apparently man can switch sensory channels to receive the necessary information about the performance of a task from another input source.

TASK TO BE LEARNED. Man's ability to switch channels of input information is directly related to the task dimension. For example, driving in a snowstorm is a more difficult task than driving in clear weather. No doubt the reader has, at one time or another, been in a situation where the weather has produced adverse driving conditions. If the windshield becomes covered with snow or mud, the driver will attempt to receive information about the car's behavior by some means other than visual. He may try to remember the road condition or he may steer the car so that one wheel is off the pavement, thus enabling him to receive tactual information through the steering wheel of the car's progress. Although his performance may deteriorate, he will attempt to switch channel input modes.

Some research studies and authors have stressed the importance of identifying the task requirements in relationship to the type and role of feedback. Fox and Levy (1969), Bourne (1966), and Armstrong (1970), all mentioned that the usefulness of various types of feedback may be task specific. Armstrong (1970) reviewed more than fifty studies dealing with feedback and perceptual motor skill learning, and concluded that the discrepancies in the various findings of these several studies may have been due to the components of the task. Thus, the usefulness of feedback types and modes may be largely task specific.

In driving a car, a great deal of visual feedback is necessary for good performance. Likewise, certain sport skills demand the presence of certain sensory inputs rather than others. Any type of aiming task calls for good visual feedback. Tasks that call for gross movements of the body demand adequate kinesthetic information. Thus when the role of feedback is discussed the stage of learning and arrival time of feedback must be considered as well as the specific task dimension.

FEEDBACK LOOPS

Feedback comes to the central processing system through the various sensory modes. Information from the sense organs—which are stimulated from outside the body and provide knowledge of events happening outside the body—is classified as *external feedback. Internal feedback* refers to those receptor organs that register or provide information regarding the action of the body itself.

Annett and Kay (1957) used the term *intrinsic feedback* to refer to information inherent in the task, i.e., information specific to that particular task. Internal feedback refers to the proprioceptive level of control.

Confusion has arisen between the terms intrinsic feedback and internal feedback. Intrinsic feedback is information "looped" to the task. Internal feedback is information arising as a consequence of one's own movement pattern. For example, the feedback information a player must process in order to hit a ball from a batting tee is different than the information processed in order to hit a pitched ball. This type of feedback is termed intrinsic feedback. In both situations of batting, the internal feedback received from the movement pattern execution may be similar, but the intrinsic feedback received because of the task differences is not the same.

Figure 7 shows an illustration of the concept of the feedback loops as Fitts (1965) displayed them. As can be seen in this illustration; loops number 1, 2, and 3 depict the internal feedback modes, while loops numbered 6, 7, and 8 show the loops concerned specifically with the task. The dynamic interplay of all the various feedback loops can be seen by the arrows which connect internal, intrinsic, and external feedback sources.

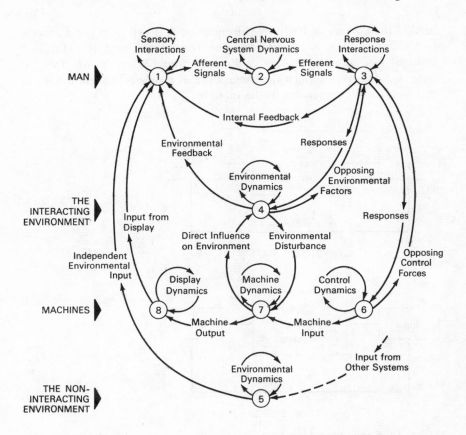

FIG. 7   ILLUSTRATION OF SOME OF THE DYNAMIC FEEDBACK LOOPS INVOLVED IN SKILLED
PERFORMANCE. THE NODES IN THE DIAGRAM REPRESENT THE FOLLOWING DYNAMIC
PROCESSES: (1) RECEPTOR, (2) CENTRAL NERVOUS SYSTEM, (3) EFFECTOR, (4) AND (5)
SOCIAL-ENVIRONMENTAL, (6) CONTROL, (7) MACHINE, AND (8) DISPLAY. (AFTER FITTS,
1962. REPRODUCED WITH PERMISSION OF JOHN WILEY & SONS, INC., NEW YORK.)

OPEN AND CLOSED LOOPS

The terms open and closed loop feedback refer to the presence or
absence of feedback in the behavioral system. In a closed loop system
there is continual feedback. An open loop system implies the absence of
feedback.

If feedback is eliminated from one source, the feedback loop is
opened. Figure 8 shows a simplified diagram of feedback and illustrates
the concept of open and closed loop feedback. An open loop system

implies the absence of feedback information. A closed loop system is one in which feedback is continuous. The reader may find it helpful to think of feedback loops as water flowing through a system of pipes. So long as the pipes are intact the water flows. If a pipe is broken, the water leaks out and never reaches its destination.

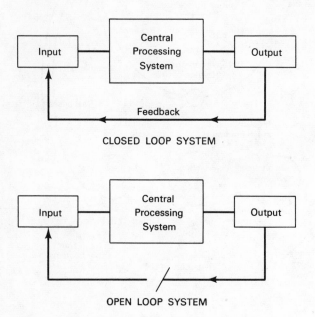

FIG. 8   OPEN AND CLOSED LOOP FEEDBACK SYSTEMS

The argument that suggests that man can operate as an open loop feedback system is based on the assumption that if man is a multiple level or hierarchical behavioral system, then perhaps he can "program" activities in advance. That is, he initiates an action and this action "runs off" to completion without feedback. This argument has not generally been accepted by cybernetic theorists because the term cybernetic itself implies the presence of some type of feedback information at all times, i.e., there is no time when there is a complete absence of feedback.

For the most part cybernetic theorists believe than man operates with continual feedback or as a closed loop system. Feedback is perhaps the most important variable to study in the cybernetic theory, and to suggest the absence of feedback is in opposition to the general cybernetic theory. Man can perhaps operate for a very short time without any feedback, but his performance rapidly deteriorates if feedback is not available.

INTERNAL LOOPS

The working of the internal loops has been of great interest to physical educators. Kinesthetic sense (or more popularly, proprioceptive sense) is one type of internal feedback. Many physical educators have studied the measurement of kinesthetic ability. Scott (1955), Slater-Hammel (1957), Wiebe (1954), and Young (1945) attempted to devise various tests to detect individual differences in kinesthetic sensitivity. They concluded that no one test can measure kinesthetic sensitivity and hence, that kinesthesis may be composed of a series of specific functions.

Conflicting results have arisen in physical education studies where specific attempts were made to increase the information obtained through the internal feedback mode of kinesthetic sense. Cox (1933) and Griffith (1931) found that emphasizing kinesthetic awareness improved learning ability in a specific task, while Coady (1950), McGrath (1947), and Roloff (1953) found that special attempts of the instructor to emphasize kinesthetic awareness did not aid in improving the ability of subjects to learn a task.

Some studies have attempted to determine the relationship between kinesthetic sensitivity and success in various sport activities. Phillips and Summers (1954) found a positive relationship between positional tests of kinesthesis and bowling ability. However, Witte (1962) found no significant relationship between ball rolling ability of elementary school children and positional measures of kinesthesis. Mumby (1953) found a significant relationship between ability to maintain a constant muscular pressure under a dynamic changing condition and wrestling ability.

Human performance psychologists have been interested in determining the role of internal feedback in the learning and executing of skills. Fitts (1951), concerned with the role of visual and proprioceptive feedback, stated:

> . . . visual control is important when an individual is learning a new perceptual motor task. As performance becomes habitual, however, it is likely that proprioceptive feedback or "feel" becomes more important (pp. 1323–24).[2]

Gagne and Fleishman (1959) stated:

> In many human motor skills, high levels of proficiency may depend more and more on internal cues as learning continues. The novice golfer checks

2 A. M. Fitts, "Engineering Psychology and Equipment Design," in S. S. Stevens, ed., *Handbook of Experimental Psychology* (New York: John Wiley & Sons, Inc., 1951). Used by permission.

his grip visually . . . lines up his club head repeatedly . . . it is only when the internal cues have been dependably sorted out that the golfer can achieve a consistent swing (p. 237).[3]

The knowledge of how internal feedback works has not yet been established, but there appear to be two main hypotheses. Lashley and Ball (1929) raised the question of whether habits are controlled by proprioceptive sense or by an intraneural mechanism. Chernikoff and Taylor (1952) conducted a study to determine proprioceptive reaction time. They reasoned that if man acted as a system in which his responses were continually guided, then such a system would need continuous information. Their results showed that proprioceptive reaction time was too slow to provide continuous information.

Gibbs (1954) argued, however, that if proprioceptive sense were not involved in continuous regulation, then there would be no feedback during continuous movements until after the movement was completed. This poses the question of whether or not proprioceptive feedback is an error-correcting mechanism during rapid movements. The evidence from Lashley (1951) and from Chernikoff and Taylor (1952) suggests that the rapidity of skilled movements precludes the possibility of point-for-point proprioceptive control. The reasoning by Gibbs, however, leads one to believe that some type of control must be going on. According to Fitts (1951) skilled movements in a continuous phase are not under continuous visual control.

GROUP INTERACTION FEEDBACK

K. U. Smith (1970) used a very descriptive term to describe feedback that occurs in groups. The term used was "social feedback yoking." For example, when two people are talking to each other the feedback loop is enlarged and the people are "yoked" together. A basketball team is "yoked" together and feedback interaction occurs among all members of the team.

Too often feedback has been thought of on an individual basis, and it is important to realize that information is gained and interpreted in different ways depending on the number of people involved. Cybernetic theory can be used to study group effectiveness. Internal feedback (verbal and nonverbal) is feedback which is processed by the various members of the group. External feedback is information received by other groups and aids in regulating the members of the group.

[3] R. M. Gagne, and E. A. Fleishman, *Psychology and Human Performance: An Introduction to Psychology* (New York: Holt, Rinehart & Winston, Inc., 1959). Used by permission.

Fitt's diagram shows group interaction feedback. His term for this type of feedback was "environmental dynamics." (see Figure 7, p. 101).

NOISE AND FEEDBACK

All forms of feedback are not intrinsically beneficial to performance. When information is detrimental to the system, it is termed "noise." The effect of noise on the system depends upon the intensity, location, and similarity of noise to helpful information. If, for example, noise enters the system from an external source (outside environment), some type of disturbance to the system will occur if the noise is sufficient or intense enough to mask other signals.

It must be remembered that man does have the ability to filter out irrelevant information or noise *if* he is able to discriminate between relevant and irrelevant information. Thus, an important technique in teaching is that of aiding the learner to discriminate between useful and nonuseful information.

Similarly, too much information, or information input can disrupt performance. An interesting study was conducted by Gilman (1967) concerning the elaboration of information feedback. The question raised in this study was: "Would students learn faster, or more, if they were given more elaborate information about their responses?" Imagine, for example, would one learn more quickly how to hit the golf ball efficiently if one could receive error information as to the exact reasons why he did not hit the ball, e.g., incorrect wrist angle, failure to build up speed, failure to shift weight, etc.? In fact, would one learn faster and more efficiently if one had a computer along side to give a very elaborate analysis of one's swing? Gilman's results suggest that the elaborate prompting and overt correction procedures may not be more effective than the less elaborate and straightforward feedback and correction procedure.

The interesting implication for physical educators is the use of the terms "straightforward feedback and correction procedures." A wealth of information or elaborate information simply overloads the individual's information channels. *Augmented feedback* should be supplied to provide positive cue corrections. Simply telling the student the ball went to the left or right, or sliced or hooked, gives him little useful information. Giving him the mechanical analysis and reasons why may provide him with too much information. The answer lies in giving the student a correctional procedure or a coaching cue that may correct the error.

Noise can occur from sources other than the teacher. For example, booing a player attempting to make a free shot in basketball may interfere with the success of his performance. Once again, the performer must learn to filter out irrelevant information.

REFERENCE PATTERNS

In all attempts to utilize feedback effectively, the performer must have an accurate reference pattern to which he can compare his response. Wiener's definition of feedback stressed the importance of error information that occurs as a result of comparison of the actual pattern to the desired pattern. For feedback to be effectively utilized, the reference pattern must be available to the learner. Perhaps this is one of the more important keys to the effective use of feedback.

Learning to perform a skill involves the establishment of a reference pattern, or a mental "image" of the correct response. It seems safe to assume that a learner will always adopt some type of reference pattern. He will perceive some standard or goal as well as some type of correct movement pattern with which to compare his responses.

Seashore and Bavelas (1941) conducted a study in which the reference level or pattern was not made clear to the subjects. They found that the subjects' errors did become consistent in spite of the fact that they were without a definite type of reference level. The subjects did make errors, but the important point is that these errors varied less as practice proceeded. Thus, without external standards by which to compare performance, the subjects apparently learned to rely on internal standards, and attempted to match previous attempts.

The subjects mentioned above can be likened to "self-taught" performers who develop an individual "style" of performance. They establish a standard as a reference point by watching others, seeing TV performances, etc. They proceed to learn to perform the skill by themselves, even though the final performance may include some subroutines an expert would consider errors. The range of variations is reduced so the performance is consistent, and we must acknowledge the fact that adjustments have been made for the "errors"; that is, even the "errors" become consistent.

There are two important considerations here for physical educators. First of all, we must acknowledge the fact that more and more performers come to us with already established movement patterns and in many cases, established sports skills. We must consider carefully the pros and cons of recommending changes.

Secondly, the difficulty of establishing reference patterns for sport skills must be recognized as a direct challenge to physical educators.

Levels of performance—beginning, intermediate, and advanced—have been used quite arbitrarily to establish abstract reference patterns for students. Too few *definite* reference patterns have been established to which a beginning player can compare his progress. Some instructors in physical education use an expert's standard for judging all levels of performance. To the beginner, an expert's standard must appear as an impossible and highly unreasonable reference pattern. What effect will such a practice have on the individual's motivation to learn?

It is extremely important to realize that in order to effectively utilize the feedback principle, the reference pattern or the desired movement response must be clear and realistic to the learner. It is also clear that the student's reference pattern *may or may not* be that of the teacher's. If there is a discrepancy between the teacher's reference pattern and that of the student, then discouragement and inadequacy will no doubt occur for both the teacher and the learner.

For example, beginning golfers are sometimes misled by the reference response of the desirable score to achieve. The only score which appears on the score card is "par." Likewise, golfers discussing scores generally refer to par. TV accounts of golf matches refer to par and subpar scores. Therefore, the reference pattern is that of how the experts score. Discouragement and disillusion can result after their first attempts to play a "real" game, unless they set realistic reference responses for golf scores.

Probably the first reference response to set for beginners who have never played before is fifteen strokes per hole. Although a score of this kind seems extremely high, compared to par, it is realistic and does allow the golfer to set progressive goals. When a golfer reaches a reference response of "ten" strokes for each hole he has made considerable progress and may be "hooked on golf."

The reference patterns can be made more realistic in another way, also. The suggestion can be made that counting square contacts with the ball and/or accurate approaching and putting movements are more important at this stage than an expert's scoring pattern. While these examples may seem quite simple and obvious, many teachers have overlooked them as realistic reference responses and/or patterns.

It is also important to determine how the learner is perceiving the desired reference pattern for the skill he is trying to learn. One method has been to ask the student to verbalize by describing what he is trying to accomplish. In this way incorrect perceptual images of a reference pattern may be determined. Verbalization may help the teacher provide information that will help the student adjust or correct his reference pattern. Also, the key to more efficient information or feedback processing on the part of the learner may be in the area of establishing logical, realistic reference patterns. Without a correct reference pattern, students can become consistent in their errors but may never be able to *correct* their errors simply because they used an incorrect reference pattern. The ability of teachers to know and recognize good reference patterns is obviously important. The teacher who can demonstrate a good or correct pattern is particularly fortunate.

IMPLICATIONS FOR TEACHING

In the field of physical education relatively little research has been reported in which specific feedback modes were utilized and in which the recording of the subjects' responses was controlled. In one sense it can be said that physical educators have studied feedback indirectly by being concerned primarily about the practical application of various kinds of feedback.

Temporal and spatial accuracy of movement is required in all sport tasks. The champion or skilled player has narrowed the "range" of error regarding the temporal and spatial requirements of the task. Each performer establishes a reference pattern in order to compare output. The difference between this reference pattern and output is the error. The difference between the "duffer" and the "champion" is the range of error. The role of the physical educator is to aid the student in correctly identifying errors and to provide new information input that may aid students reduce the range of error.

Most tasks in sports require the performer to remember the ideal pattern, i.e., to produce the movement pattern the learner must rely on memory. A few researchers are beginning to study the most effective training method for aiding learners to remember the specific movement pattern.

Manual guidance has been studied as to its effectiveness in aiding learners to produce memorized movement patterns. Lincoln (1956), studying the effect of different modes of receiving specific error information, used manual guidance as a means of teaching subjects to turn a wheel at a certain rate. Subjects in one group received verbal information about the errors they made while attempting to turn the wheel of a machine at a specified rate. Subjects in another group grasped the knob of the handwheel, and then the wheel turned automatically at a rate equivalent to their average error rate on the previous trial. Subjects in the third group received no direct error information. They practiced by grasping the handwheel while it was turned automatically at the standard rate they were to learn. The results indicated that subjects in group one and two, who received some type of error information, were superior during training to those subjects in group three who received no direct error information. The criterion tests consisted of subject attempting to produce the same rate without the aid of any external feedback. Final performances for all three groups did not vary significantly.

Armstrong (1970) investigated the use of manual guidance; his results indicated that manual guidance was not useful for the eventual production of a memorized pattern. Armstrong studied five different conditions for the training of a tracking task. The criterion test was to produce the practiced tracking task from memory. Subjects in condition number five had their arm guided through the movement pattern. As would be expected they made the fewest errors during practice. However, when they attempted to produce the pattern from memory, they scored higher, that is, made more errors than any of the other groups.

Armstrong's (1970) experiments reproduced similar learning conditions as those investigated by the author (Robb 1966). In Robb's and Armstrong's studies, laboratory equipment and techniques were used to score a subject's ability to learn a specified movement. During training and testing, a measure of mean error that occurred during each trial as subjects attempted to match an output signal with an input signal was obtained. Both studies utilized a pursuit tracking test. The data were analyzed in terms of the subject's ability to utilize the information gained from varying schedules of terminal and concurrent feedback.

The criterion test in both studies consisted of performance of the arm movement pattern without explicit visual feedback. In other words, the question being investigated was, "After a skill becomes highly practiced, can subjects perform the pattern relying mainly on memory?"

Robb's study was designed to present methods of training which simulated various known methods used in the teaching of physical education activities. Subjects in one group were trained with the method sometimes termed "slow controlled rehearsals." In this method students go through the movement pattern of a skill slowly before practicing the required performance at the standard rate. By paralleling this method in a laboratory setting, evidence indicated that this method did not aid students to learn a memorized movement pattern. In fact, the student's acquisition of skill may be hindered. It should be noted, however, that the movement sequence used in this study did not involve as highly complex a patterning of movement as is needed in many sport skills. It is possible that further study may show that the use of slow practice in a movement involving a complex sequence may be beneficial. If a student is having difficulty with the sequential ordering of the subroutines, then slow controlled practice may prove helpful.

Robb's study simulated the "kinesthetic approach" to teaching physical education activities in two of her groups. The so-called kinesthetic method attempts to develop each student's awareness of the "feel" of the movement. The subjects in these two groups were trained without visual feedback. When the subjects were forced to rely only on memory and internal cues during the training sessions, their error scores were higher than the error scores of any other group. Whenever anyone executes a movement, proprioceptors are being used. The necessity of using specific devices to bring awareness of proprioception to the conscious level seems questionable. The enforced use of proprioceptors alone did not aid the subjects in this study to perform the movement pattern better than subjects learning via other schedules.

Demonstration is commonly used to teach sport skills. The students passively participate by watching a skilled performance of the movement before they attempt the movement. The subjects who engaged in passive participation followed by active practice did not gain skill during training as much as those subjects who had continual active visual practice. Demonstrations may play a role in explaining the objective or executive plan of the task to the learner, but passive participation does not provide subjects with error information or feedback.

The results of this study showed that none of the practice conditions produced significantly better performances on criterion test. The conditions of slow controlled practice and passive participation were definitely inferior methods when compared to the other conditions. The trend indicated that the group that received concurrent visual feedback was receiving the most beneficial information.

Armstrong (1970), investigating the concurrent visual feedback trend reported by Robb, found this trend to be misleading. He reported that presenting error information concurrently did not lead to developing any better memory for the production of the particular pattern of movement than did normal trial and error learning. His results suggest that the best training method for producing a pattern of movement from memory is practice on the task itself, including much terminal information available immediately after performance. The fact that concurrent information training methods did not enhance learning resulted from the fact that receiving terminal information was extremely compatible with the task or final objective.

The results of both of these studies appear to point to the importance of feedback specific to the task. Concurrent feedback should not be regarded as an inherently poor method of instruction. Indeed, if the task calls for utilizing concurrent feedback, then such information is vital for successful performance. In most skills, visual feedback is very important. The tracking movements of the eyes are essential for success in many sport skills. Information from this visual mode is received both concurrently and terminally. Apparently each training method must be specifically arranged and planned according to the specific task requirements.

THE FUTURE OF FEEDBACK

If one were to predict the future of feedback, it would seem that it is probably going to be one of the most important areas of study in education and teaching. The feedback now used in teaching sport skills is largely external information feedback of the terminal type. As teachers of skill we generally give information about our assessment of a student's movement pattern. We correct form or mechanical efficiency according to our preconceived idea of the way a movement should look. Although the type of terminal feedback may vary from a subjective appraisal to a numerical grade, it nevertheless is *our* subjective appraisal of a student's movement patterns. This is more properly labeled teacher-determined feedback. It is based on the assumption that the teacher knows what the student needs. In very few instances do teachers allow a student to determine what he wants. In many cases teachers are unaware of any type of feedback other than knowledge of results.

To some, the feedback principle, which is based on a computer analogy, seems cold and inhuman. Although computors are not human, the reader must remember that the computor analogy is only that—an analogy. It is used to help explain the concept and the power of feedback. It does not logically follow that in using the feedback principle, teaching will become less human. If anything, an understanding of the feedback principle will make teaching more enjoyable.

Nor does the recent interest in machine and technology mean that the teacher will be relegated to a less important role. This myth has been perpetuated because of teachers' fears that they will be replaced by a machine; it is misleading and unfounded. Machines can be used to aid the teacher. One has only to study man's capacities and limitations to realize that man is capable of doing many things a machine is not capable of doing. One of the more important things that man can do is make decisions—machines cannot. But man can use machines to help him make better decisions. For example, a storage system machine which classifies information and allows information to be retrieved can be extremely helpful in making decisions. Man's memory is poor in comparison to a machine's. Therefore, man makes decisions with a limited memory capacity. If machines were used to aid man's memory, better decisions might be made. Wouldn't it be nice if we had a machine to record and store the data about all our students? We could then make a decision about a student's learning program with the aid of a machine storage bank rather than relying on our own limited memory capacity.

The potential use of the feedback principle is fascinating. The book *Education and Ecstasy* by George Leonard portrays the educational system of the year 2000. Children aided by electronical hardware became empathetic adults. There was no greater educational goal in the year 2000 than human understanding. The power and principles of feedback were more fully understood and there was increased knowledge of group interaction. The information available from enlarged feedback loops (which occurs when two or more people interact) was more accurately interpreted and processed. Increased knowledge of feedback can only lead to an increased knowledge of human interaction and understanding.

Leonard pictures various domes of learning in his book. The "quiet dome" is where all the qualities of tranquility and peace are experienced. The "sensory dome" is where one learns to sort out incoming sensory bombardment. The "water dome" is where interaction with water and gravity is solved by the learner. The "body dome" is where body sensory feedback devices are available to help the learner consciously control his body.

Lacking in Leonard's educational ecstasy is what might be termed the "skill dome." Using Leonard's approach let us proceed to the "skill dome." Inside we find individual practice rooms equipped with information-producing devices. Each child practices by himself or interacts with others in order to improve movement patterns. By the age of twelve, the movement patterns of each child are so well controlled that the child moves with grace and efficiency. Each in tune with his body, each comfortable in his own skin.

One particular practice room attracts our attention. The skill that the child is learning involves balancing himself on a board similar to the old bongo boards. This task, called a compensatory tracking task, involves balancing on an unstable platform. In olden days this task was used in motor-learning experiments and was called a stabliometer. In the year 2000 four-year-olds learn this task in about fifteen minutes. They do so with the aid of several feedback devices. An oscillograph records and displays visual information regarding tilt and error. The principle of feedforward takes care of the human time lag in feedback processing. Anticipatory information is available if the learner desires. The learner can use increased tactual or intrinsic feedback. All feedback information is student determined.

The children, having previously learned to control exact muscular contraction and relaxation with the aid of other feedback devices, have no problem with fatigue. Perfection of the bongo board task leads naturally to perfection of body movements on the balance beam, and other gymnastic apparatus, as well as balance on the "rovers." The rovers are machines called "cybernetic rovers" that travel on water, land, and snow. The forerunners of these machines, the snowmobiles and dune buggies, were replaced several years ago by cybernetic rovers which eliminated the noise and pollution of the older machines.

Riding a cybernetic rover involves a combination of balance, feedback processing, and gravitational movements. It is not surprising to see games of tag played on these machines. The object is for one player to interrupt the feedback information of the other person by means of low-intensity laser rays. The "interrupted person" must quickly "plug in" another feedback information device in order to remain in motion.

The older games involving balls, physical contact, and aggression are not very popular. As Metheny (1968) predicted, the games of man and machine intertacting with nature are the games of the future.

BACK TO THE PRESENT

Are these dreams possible? Lang's work (see *Psychology Today,* Oct., 1970) on automatic conditioning and voluntary control of the autonomic nervous system makes us realize that the ideas of Leonard's body dome are not so fantastic, but almost a reality. The entire concept of Lang's research is based on the feedback loop principle.

Kamiya (1968) is working with "brain training" or alpha control. In his work subjects can learn to produce alpha brain waves if visual feedback is provided by an EEG reading. Alpha waves are brain waves that have a rhythm of eight to twelve cycles per second. Given the proper feedback, an individual can seemingly learn to "read" his own body systems.

Change has been occurring at a greater rate in this century than at any other time. This was the point raised by Alvin Toffler in his 1970 best seller *Future Shock.* According to Toffler, the future will shock us if we are not psychologically prepared for change. How does one prepare for the future and change? Although Toffler doesn't mention the term feedback, he was indeed speaking of the feedback principle when he pointed out that individuals can be helped to adapt if they are provided with advance information about what will occur. Advance information, or anticipatory feedback is what Toffler was talking about. Once again the principle of feedback becomes an important concept for the future.

SUMMARY

Feedback has many ramifications and implications for the learning of skills. The use of the terms reward, reinforcement, and knowledge of results are inadequate for describing the term feedback.

Feedback plays the role of motivating, reinforcing, and/or regulating behavior and is one of the stronger variables controlling behavior. It is difficult, in many cases, to distinguish between the motivation, reinforcing, and regulating effects of feedback.

The term reinforcement implies that a response is made, and that the response is reinforced through some particular means of supplying information. In terms of theoretical considerations, reinforcement is thought of as drive reduction or the development of habit strength. Teachers are generally concerned with the operational characteristics of reinforcement rather than the theoretical constructs, that is, with the processes involved in presenting certain reinforcers to increase desired responses.

There is general agreement among educators and researchers that feedback does play a motivating role. The mere approval or disapproval such as nodding the head, saying "good," or even grunting disapproval can serve to modify behavior. The relationship between the experimenter and the subject, between the teacher and the student, or between the coach and the player appears to affect the usefulness of reinforcement.

There is a need to distinguish not only the role of feedback, but also its type, mode, and process. Terms such as internal, intrinsic, augmented, and concurrent aid in the determination of the locus of feedback as well as the temporal arrival of information. The term information feedback has been more acceptable to many experts than reinforcement feedback. In most cases, information feedback is externally supplied and therefore is augmented information of the concurrent or terminal variety. Information feedback aids each learner to determine how closely his pattern of movement achieves the desired pattern. Internal feedback or sensory feedback is a result of the processing of information gained through the action of the body itself.

In all cases, a reference pattern or desired pattern must be determined by the experimenter, the teacher, and the learner. Helping individuals achieve realistic reference patterns is the role of the teacher. The teacher also plays the role of providing certain types of feedback information. Take, for example, the basketball teacher who explains and demonstrates the jump shot, and then has the students perform the pattern of the jump shot. He is aiding the establishment of a reference response pattern. The feedback available after the students attempt to reproduce the desired pattern is largely of an internal nature (except as the teacher may supplement the information or augment the information).

How could the teacher augment information for students learning the pattern of the jump shot in basketball? He could guide the students through the intricate wrist action, or could shout "now" when the time is right to release the ball. Action shot pictures could be taken of the student executing the jump shot; movies or video tape replays of the execution could be provided. These are all forms of augmented feedback.

There is a need for further study concerning the most efficient methods for training individuals to perform a memorized pattern. Many sport skills demand this type of behavior. Modes and types of feedback need to be defined and described. Task specific feedback, especially, should be identified for its role in the execution of various skilled movements.

It is recognized to be effectively skillful one must, first of all, possess good effectors and second, the performance of these effectors must be properly monitored back to the central processing system. All readings must be combined and coordinated with other information arriving from the various sense organs if the individual is to be able to increase the effectiveness of his output.

The possible educational uses of feedback in the future are exciting. A child in the future may be able to learn not only to control his body, but also to answer the many existential questions regarding himself—he will actually "come alive" with feedback!

CHAPTER EIGHT

SPORT
CLASSIFICATION
SYSTEMS

Is the basketball coach talking about the same movement as the
gymnastic expert? Does the swimming coach confer about the same type
of task as the football coach? Does the biomechanics expert have a different language than the exercise physiologist or motor-learning expert?
Are students confused about description of various movement patterns?
Do we understand what we're talking about when we speak of skilled
movement?

The answer to these questions basically is "no." Various sport
experts do not communicate effectively with each other because the
commonalities within the various sports have not been identified and
categorized. Communication is possible. Commonalities do exist. Communication can be improved provided a reasonable classification system
can be developed.

Biology has used a classification system for years. The familiar terms
of kingdom, phylum, class, order, family, genus, species, and variety have
been used to systematically arrange animals and plants into categories. Bloom et al. have developed a method for classifying educational objectives.[1] They suggest that a third area, the psychomotor
domain, be investigated. While the existence of this third domain has

[1] Two handbooks have been written: B. S. Bloom et al., *Taxonomy of Educa-
tional Objectives: Handbook I: Cognitive Domain* (New York: David McKay Company,
Inc., 1956); and D. R. Kratwohl et al., *Taxonomy of Educational Objectives: Handbook
II: Affective Domain* (New York: David McKay Company, Inc., 1964).

been recognized, little work has been accomplished in classifying it. Simpson (1966–67) did some work in the psychomotor domain and attempted to classify psychomotor skills using the same pattern as originally proposed by Bloom and others (see Appendix A, p. 156).

Jewett, Jones, Luneke, and Robinson (1971) have recognized the need for a taxonomy for curriculum planning. Their work is a first step in solving the long needed classification in the "movement" domain of learning. Their hierarchical view of classifying the processes involved in all types of movements should serve as an aid to writing and clarifying objectives of physical education.

Bloom used the word taxonomy to refer to any classification system based on principles or general laws. A taxonomy is developed by applying a consistent set of characteristics in order to classify components. If general laws or principles were applied in such a way that skilled movements involved in sports were classified into various categories, then communication, curriculum planning, and evaluation might be conducted more effectively. The major importance of a taxonomy is that it aids in the understanding of the task and hence directly affects the structuring of the learning environment.

In this chapter several possibilties for developing a taxonomy for skills will be presented. Although each taxonomy has certain advantages, each also has limitations, and the task of developing a taxonomy which will fit certain predictable criteria is still to be accomplished.

THE CRITERIA FOR A TAXONOMY

Fitts (1965) suggested that a taxonomy should identify learning rate, performance level, and individual differences. Bloom, mainly concerned with the specification of educational objectives, attempted to base each classification system on a specific principle or a consistent set of principles. His classification system gave a more comprehensive understanding of the terms cognitive, affective, and psychomotor learning. For the specification of various objectives and evaluative procedures, Bloom's work is extremely helpful. His statements of objectives in terms of behavioral characteristics provide a more accurate evaluation of the learning process.

Melton (1964) suggested that a taxonomy or a classification scheme should specify the tasks humans learn by describing, identifying, and relating them to other tasks. However, a relationship between the science of learning, the science of psychology, and the technology of educational methods is lacking. The teacher can find little help in the theoretical knowledge and descriptive categories such as discrimination learning, tracking, concept formation, etc. Similarly, each term must be fully defined within the context of experiments for clarity. Communication problems are inherent in most research studies.

Perhaps one of the more important uses of a taxonomy, and thus an important criterion, is that a classification system should be closely related to methodology and decisions about the preferred method of training or of learning a task. This type of classification helps the teacher to plan. Methods of instruction can be based on behavioral objectives. A task taxonomy should give the teacher a perspective of the emphasis to be placed on certain behavioral objectives. What specific objectives does the task call for? What movements are involved? What makes the task difficult? A task taxonomy should answer these questions as well as others.

TRADITIONAL CLASSIFICATION SYSTEMS

Traditionally, a common system used to classify sport tasks has been to use the terms team, individual, and dual sports. This classification is based on the criterion of the number of participants involved in a certain sport. The limitation of this classification system is that it only informs us of the number of people involved and tells very little about individual differences, learning rate, or performance levels.

Some studies have attempted to identify the personality traits of individuals as related to participation in individual, dual, or team sports. However, as far as specifying learning rate in terms of methods to be employed, or performance levels in terms of curriculum planning, this type of classification system has severe limitations.

Performance levels have been distinguished in sport tasks by classifying a player as a beginner, an intermediate, or advanced. The most serious limitation of this classification system is that the identification of each category (beginning, intermediate, or advanced,) is dependent upon one's previous frame of reference. Skill involves the dynamic interplay of the receptor-effector-feedback systems and cannot necessarily be labeled as beginning, intermediate, or advanced. Skill can be defined simply as the accomplishment of a certain movement. The terms beginning, intermediate, and advanced have proved useful in specifying the amount of prior instruction in physical education classes. However, this type of classification system is based on the principle of previous experience rather than actual level of proficiency.

Some interest has been generated by kinesiologists and biomechanists in a system of classification based on the speed and/or duration of a movement. For example, the terms slow, ballistic, and fixated have been used to describe the rate of movement during the execution of a skill.

As early as 1905, Stetson reported an experiment in which a record of the "up and down" beat movements of a baton were recorded. Stetson was particularly interested in the beat-stroke rhythm. He reported that rhythm is dynamic and consists of actual movements which may or may not be perceived as actual movements of particular joints. His analysis of the movement cycle of a beat portrayed a contraction of the muscle at the beginning of the motion, followed by a relaxation during the latter half of the movement together with a contraction of the antagonistic muscle group which arrested the limb.

In later studies, Stetson labeled this type of movement a ballistic or loose rapid movement. Additional movement definitions developed by Stetson and McDill (1923) were:

Fixation: in which groups of opposing muscles are contracted against each other or hold still movements (posture)

Slow: movements in which groups of opposing muscles are contracted against each other, but with uneven tension so that change of position of moving members results or "controlled" movement

Rapid: movement which cannot be changed at every point in its course. The movement must be determined before the actual movement begins. (a) Movement in which there is tension in all the opposing muscle groups throughout the movement or the positive muscle group and antagonistic muscle group maintain a tension against each other. (Stiff rapid movements) (b) Movement in which the contraction of the positive muscle group relaxes long before the end of the movement. (Ballistic movement or "loose" rapid movement)

Hartson (1939) distinguished between movements that either involved slow tension or were ballistic. He included fixation and slow controiled movements under slow tension. Ballistic movements were those that were either "stiff" rapid, or "loose" rapid.

Using the above classification system, a specific task can be described as containing a certain type of movement. For example, posture can be described as fixation. This type of classification system also proves useful in describing, to a certain extent, the learning rate. Stetson and McDill (1923) pointed out that in progressing from slow to rapid movements, the person is substituting a single movement for several movements. When a beginner first learns to type, for example, he puts the finger on the key, then presses down. As he becomes better at typing, the placing and striking of the key become one stroke.

Smith and Smith (1966) suggested that movements can be meaningfully classified as either postural, transport, or manipulative types of movement. According to Smith and Smith, the advantages of this kind of a classification system are: (1) that different types of movements can be postulated as being controlled by separate brain centers and thus the location of sensory information for each of the movements can be better defined; (2) that there is a relationship between the types of movements and the periods of human growth and development as well as a comparison available between movements humans can make and movements made by lower vertebrates; (3) that experimental analysis and research can be more readily understood by explaining the types of movements involved in the task the subject is asked to perform; and (4) that a more meaningful framework is provided to aid in the understanding of spatial orientation and movements of the body.

Specifically, this taxonomy states that all the movements man performs can be divided into either postural movements, transporting movements, or manipulative movements. In postural movements gravity plays an important part and the movement is controlled by the medulla, the cerebellum, and the midbrain. Smith and Smith believe postural movements are the first to be developed in humans. The mechanisms that control postural components are those that provide a vertically oriented or up-down reference system.

Transporting movements propel the body through space, and a right-left reference system is extremely important. The regulation of the right and left limbs through bilaterally organized feedback loops is a consideration in this type of movement. Smith and Smith used the term "free space" to describe movement in space where gravity is the main component to overcome.

In addition to movements in free space, there are also movements in "hard" space. Movements in hard space are for the purpose of manipulating objects in space. Thus, the contours, surfaces, and object characteristics occurring in hard space become important considerations.

It is difficult to separate movements in hard space from movements in free space. Although a runner moves through free space, he must be concerned with the type of surface underneath, also. Running in the sand becomes a different type of movement than running on a concrete pavement. Transport movements require one to process information obtained from both hard and free space.

Manipulative movements involve fine and gross manipulation of objects. Feedback is received from the tactual mode or from the "feel" of the object as well as from visual modes.

Skilled responses in sports may contain a combination of the three types of components of movements—postural, transport, and manipulative. The location of the feedback loops and the type of information being processed according to the type of movement component greatly affects one's ability to accurately and successfully perform skilled movements. Feedback that occurs in manipulative movements arises mainly from external receptors. Postural movements depend a great deal on internal feedback. Transport movements depend on spatial orientation and directional characteristics.

It is obvious that this approach has great benefit for classifying movements and specifying feedback modes. In fact, Smith and Smith's classification system is similar to the traditional method of slow, fixation, and ballistic type movements previously discussed. The added information of the feedback processing locality makes this taxonomy more attractive than the older classification system.

RECENT TAXONOMIES

More recent classifications systems have been developed by human performance theorists working them in the area of skill acquisition. Those to be reported are: Knapp's classification system based on Poulton's work, Fitts's levels of difficulties, and Vanek and Cratty's abilities and games categories. A description of each taxonomy is presented and examples of the tasks given that are classified under each system.

KNAPP'S CONTINUUM OF SKILLS

Knapp (1963) adapted Poulton's (1957) classification of skills and suggested that all sport tasks can be arranged on a continuum by identifying whether or not the skills involved in the sports are "closed skills" or "open skills." A continuum was suggested since many sport tasks contain both open and closed skills.

Poulton's classification system is based on an examination of the environment in which the skill is to be performed. Is the environment predictable and relatively unchanging, or is the environment unpredictable and constantly in a state of flux? His classification system was based on the assumption that learning a skill involves the determination of patterns of movements needed to regulate and adjust to the environment. Poulton labeled skills performed in a relatively stable environment as *closed skills*. If the environment is highly unpredictable and constantly changing, one needs *open skills* so that he can adjust to and/or regulate the environment.

Our environment contains objects in space to which the performer must be constantly adjusting. If we can predict with a fair amount of certainty that an object will be in a particular space the majority of the time, a different type of movement pattern is needed than to adjust to an environment where the objects are moving in space and are unpredictable. The former type of movement needed is a "closed skill" while the latter is an "open skill." Objects that move in space have not only a spatial quality but also a temporal quality. Thus, open skills require the performer to adjust to or regulate an environment containing objects that have a spatial/temporal quality. Closed skills require the performer to adjust to or regulate an environment in which the objects have only spatial nature.

The type of a classification system being discussed here suggests that different movement patterns are necessary, depending upon the environment. Certainly it is obvious that a different movement pattern is necessary to go around a parked car (spatial) as opposed to a moving car (spatial/temporal). In the case of the parked car, the object has spatial qualities and it is highly predictable as to the location of the object in space. A moving car requires the use of movement patterns based on anticipating the movement of the car in space and time.

OPEN SKILLS. In order to determine if a performer needs to utilize an open skill it is necessary to examine the task components and the relative state of the environment when the task is performed. Any sport task that has objects that move in space and that requires a spatial/temporal adjustment on the part of the performer demands open skills. In order to successfully adapt to the environment, the performer must anticipate the possible time of occurrence or arrival of objects and must adjust to the movement of those objects. Catching, batting, or stroking moving balls in baseball, basketball, softball, tennis, and volleyball call for the use of open skills. Dodging a moving opponent in basketball or soccer requires the use of open skills. In each of the above examples, the performer must learn to regulate an environment which is constantly changing both temporally and spatially. An adjustment to a changing environment must occur continually. Sports, which demand movements by the performer in accordance with the location of a moving object in space, demand the use of open skills.

If one accepts the basic assumptions of this type of classification system, the implications for teaching are extensive. Since an open skill is used to regulate a constantly changing environment, it *demands the absence of stereotyped movements.* Stereotyped movements are not useful because the chances of an object being in the same place at the same time in open sports are limited. What are the odds of always receiving a pass in basketball in the same place at the same time? When one considers all the possible places on a basketball court, as well as all the possible combinations of players, it is obvious that the identical movement pattern in catching or passing the ball is seldom repeated. Instead the player must learn to anticipate objects (ball, teammates, and opponents) in time and space, and adjust his movements to theirs.

Since open skills call for constantly changing movement patterns, one must learn sport tasks that call for open skills in a constantly changing environment. The structuring of the learning environment must simulate the environment in which the skill will be performed. It may *not* be advantageous to practice the same movement pattern over and over again in isolation until it is mastered. It may be much more advantageous to practice open skills in relation to use. Fixed, rigid movement patterns may hinder the successful accomplishment of the goal in open type sport tasks. Open skills demand capacities of the performer such as adaptability, flexibility, and anticipation. The learning environment should be structured to encourage the learners to exercise adaptability, adjustability, and anticipation.

The major source of feedback for performers who participate in tasks which call for open skills is obtained from the external environment. Teachers of games and sports should realize that students need help to become aware of the information that is available from the game environment. There are a variety of sources as well as several types of information that will, if the student can increase his awareness, improve his "game sense" and make him a better player.

The various senses provide a wealth of usable information and vision is especially important. Students should be encouraged to be aware of their range of vision both laterally and vertically. Peripheral vision is often the difference between being successful or unsuccessful in evading an opponent; it is usually the extra factor in timing a pass to a moving teammate and in providing information about background maneuvers of teammates and opponents.

There are several kinds of information about the physical and mechanical properties of objects and players that, if known in advance, can be applied to information available from the external environment. The player who recognizes possible patterns of rebound for various types of balls and who knows the effect of various types of spins on the rebound pattern can improve his effectiveness in game play. A tennis player receiving a serve, or returning a chop or a smash; and a basketball player making a lay-up or positioning himself to control a rebound are two such examples. Knowledge of the idiosyncrasies or play styles of opponents gained through observation or scouting reports may prepare a player to recognize patterns of movement during play that enable him to be effective in countermoves. Strategies of placement—both ball and player placement—should be emphasized in teaching open skills and sports rather than emphasizing stereotyped movement patterns that may never be used in an actual game situation.

The learner who becomes aware of information coming to him from the external environment has achieved only part of what he needs to be successful in sports requiring open skills. He must also be able to select the most important bits of information from all that are available. If he were to try to process all of it, the channels would be overloaded and he would be unable to cope with the situation. The person who is unable to master the selection process (mastery usually comes from experience in playing) may never make a good performer in sports requiring open skills.

Proponents of the movement education approach to skill learning are, whether they realize it or not, helping students learn to perform open skills in an environment that provides a wealth of external information. Although students are encouraged to explore their own capabilities (internal environment), there is no stereotyped pattern or sequence, no set way to perform. Students are encouraged to develop a "style" of their own, provided the resulting performance satisfies the criteria established by the teacher. Teachers who use the movement education approach, problem-solving approach, or any one of several other "open-ended" approaches to skill learning, should also provide feedback on *quality* of movement. Teachers should be aware of the different classifications (open and closed) in order to ensure the accomplishment of task objectives.

Physical educators who accept the "lead-up game" approach to teaching sports are, in a sense, seeking to control the amount of information to be processed from the game environment. Relatively simple games that lead to progressively more complex games, provide varying amounts of game information. Players learning to assess simple concepts of player relationships and play formations, gradually increase their ability to handle information available during play—provided, of course, the teacher has helped players learn the meanings of what they observe. Players do not acquire "game sense" by merely "going through the motions" of a game; i.e., participation without meaning does not provide a learning situation.

Knapp (1963) proposed that open skills are more likely taught by methods found in Gestalt learning theory, while closed skills use methods based on stimulus-response or association theory. However, the key to the effective use of open and closed skills may lie in the proper processing of feedback information. In the situation of open and closed skills being discussed here, the teacher must identify the critical components involved in each type of task. (See chapter 8 for a discussion of task analysis.)

CLOSED SKILLS. Skills executed in an environment in which objects are relatively stable, static, and unchanging call for a closed form of behavior. Objects are not moving in space and are therefore stable. Sport tasks using closed skills include gymnastics, diving, various track and field events such as high jump, javelin, swimming, bowling, free-throw shooting, and golf. In these sports the objects acted upon are not moving and the performer does not have to make periodic adjustments to moving objects. *A closed skill utilizes a stereotyped movement pattern.* A habitual repetition of the same or nearly same movement pattern is essential for success.

The performer of a closed skill task must learn to repeat a selected movement pattern with as little variation as possible, and must also learn to eliminate external influences. The objective of the sport requires the use of a set of prescribed techniques and the best performer is generally the indivdual who can repeat as nearly as possible the prescribed movement pattern. The golfer, for example, attempts to "groove" his swing. He knows that the ball will always be a certain distance from his stance and that it will not move. The balance beam is always the same width and does not move in space. Therefore, the gymnast's task is to move in a preestablished pattern across the beam. The diving board is adjusted so that the diver has the same tension available for each dive. The conditions for the high jumpers are consistent so that performers can perfect their patterns of movement.

Sport tasks that demand closed skills are often evaluated for perfection of execution. Gymnastic judges evaluate the various patterns of movement executed for each event, e.g., the vault over the horse. Sometimes performers must demonstrate set movements, known as compulsory routines, before performing individual routines they developed. There are some exceptions to this and not all closed skills are judged according to how one looks. Golf, for example, does not have this quality of evaluation. In contrast, sport tasks demanding open skills are more apt to be judged on the basis of some more objective means, such as, "Which team scored the most goals."

Since it is extremely important to build stereotyped movements in closed skills, the formation of habits is emphasized. The learning situation should be structured in such a way that desired responses will occur. Drilling the desired response is important to establish consistency or reliability of the desired response. As a general rule, however, the performer of a closed skill must concentrate on what he is doing, exclude external distractions, and repeat the same performance over and over with the patience of Job. For these reasons, the top performer of a closed sport skill may exhibit different personality characteristics than the top performer in open sport skills.

Speculations of personality variables make interesting discussions. Equally interesting and controversial is whether persons with certain personality characteristics are attracted by certain types of sports, or whether the sport reinforces the development of selected personality variables. Some will theorize that athletes in closed skill sports are more self-centered and less inclined to make good teachers. They may be capable coaches but the better teachers must interpret external information—including interaction with people.

The most important feedback for the individual to learn to process in closed skills arrives through the internal feedback loops. Proprioceptor feedback, unfortunately, is one of the most difficult for the beginner to process effectively. Awareness of body position and the location of the body in space—especially in relationship to stable objects, changes of center of gravity, points of balance, etc.—are the kinds of information the performer must learn to identify and process.

The "kinesthetic approach" to learning motor skills is more appropriate to learning closed skills than open skills. Interestingly enough, research done a few decades ago—on the "kinesthetic approach" versus the "traditional approach"—made no attempt to categorize the types of movement patterns before comparing the effectiveness of the two methods in helping students learn the skills being investigated.

The same was true of physical education research studies on whole versus part versus whole-part-whole, etc. It is quite possible that average performers may acquire complex closed skills by devoting attention to individual critical subroutines before attempting to combine them into a complete performance. On the other hand, progressive goals may be the most effective way for the majority of inexperienced students to master complex open skills. If so, the teacher involved in open skills must develop a sequence of experiences. The teacher of closed skills must select critical subroutines and develop interesting practice sessions to avoid boredom until it is time to combine the subroutines into a performance.

Probably the most essential performance of the teacher during the practice of closed skills is to provide terminal feedback, including knowledge of results, because self-analysis is especially difficult—in fact, it is nearly impossible for the beginner. To ask a beginning performer how it feels, or did it feel good, may be the wrong question because what "feels good," is usually what is familiar—whether it is correct or not. How many times teachers have heard, ". . . but it feels terrible!"

Probably the most beneficial aid in learning closed skills is to view oneself while performing. This provides a form of feedback concerning the action of the body itself that is not subject to the interpretation of someone else. Films of individuals are valuable and provide motivation as well. The major drawback is the time needed to develop the film. With a polaroid sequence camera, some portions of a performance can be seen almost immediately following the performance. However, with this method one can only "spot-check" or "sample" the performance. The instant replay video tape process is probably the best answer to the shortcomings of the other two techniques and enables both student and teacher to study the details of execution. But this technique may be time consuming and, therefore, does not lend itself to mass use. In other words, there is no real substitute for a good teacher.

OPEN-CLOSED-OPEN SKILLS. Knapp (1963), in adapting Poulton's classification of skills, suggested a continuum rather than a dichotomy. In other words, Knapp realized the existence of some sport tasks that are neither open skills nor closed skills. An example that will demonstrate the problem is that of skiing. The individual skiing alone on a small slope of consistent grade has only himself to contend with in that he attempts to execute each maneuver using the same internal and mechanical principles. However, when the slope is crowded (as it generally is), or the terrain varies from gentle to steep angles and includes several different snow conditions (from a hard-packed surface or wind crust to soft or slushy snow), skiing becomes an open skill. The skier now must process environmental information in addition to processing the internal information normally required in skiing. Anyone who doubts that this type of transformation occurs in skiing should compare the performance of the average skier executing parallel turns to both sides on normal terrain with his performance of turns on terrain filled with large moguls.

Several other sports must be listed in the borderline area between open and closed skills. Readers are encouraged to identify other sports whose characteristics change as the skills are performed in different contexts.

What about lifesaving or synchronized swimming? Does the classification change when swimmers compete in races? Does long distance running need to be reclassified when the event is a race? Suppose the race is a cross-country event? Is canoeing an open or closed skill? How about white water canoeing?

The point is that the requirements of a task must be examined in order to develop the most effective teaching procedure. While no closed skill becomes an open skill simply by changing the setting in which it is performed, the teacher's emphasis on certain aspects of the performance can be helpful to the motivated learner.

SUMMARY OF OPEN AND CLOSED SKILLS. The classification of a skill as open or closed can greatly affect the subsequent methods of instruction.

If a teacher classifies a sport as using mainly closed skills, his method of teaching will differ from a teacher who classifies the same sport as one using open skills.

In discussing this problem, Knapp (1963) used an example from tennis. She suggested that some tennis instructors classify the game of tennis as being composed of set strokes which must be practiced until the correct pattern of movement is achieved. In other words, these instructors have delegated the skills used in tennis to the closed category. Instruction methods would then consist of continual practice on selected strokes until the movement patterns had been perfected. The performer would spend hours of practice on the forehand drive, hitting the ball first from a self-bounce and progressing to practice hits and rallying against the backboard. The primary emphasis would be on reproducing the same movement strokes each time.

On the other hand, a teacher who classifies the skills in tennis as largely open would attempt to create an awareness of the changing environment in the game of tennis. The same method of stroking the ball from a self-drop and progressing to practice hits from the backboard or ballboy would probably be employed, but for a relatively brief period of time. Emphasis would be placed instead upon results achieved with the ball rather than on form of execution. Anticipation, location of self in relation to the ball, ball rebound, placement and strategy would receive greater attention than the execution of the movement pattern; except as the movement pattern limits the effectiveness of the resultant action on the ball.

Viewing pictures of the performer's movement pattern would stress attention to the movement pattern itself in closed skill instruction. If on the other hand the skills are classified as open, then learning to adjust one's own movement pattern in accordance with ball placement as well as knowledge of ball angle for returns would be emphasized rather than stereotyped movements.

Similarly the teacher who classifies the technique of spiking in volleyball as a closed skill, will concentrate on selected movement patterns of the execution of the spike rather than help the learner process external feedback information available from the game situation. Processing external feedback will aid the spiker to adjust his movements to the ball.

Open skills call for methods of instruction that aid the student in dealing with an unpredictable series of events. The squash player must learn to judge where the ball will rebound. A player may use two hands on the racquet, because it is more important to return the ball than to use an "acceptable" stroking technique. More work and study must be done to aid players in developing open skills.

In addition to influencing methods of instruction, open and closed skill classification affects evaluative techniques. Since habitual patterns of movement are the desired objective in closed skills, methods of grading should be based on how the performer looks. However, in open skills the player is constantly *changing* movement patterns. The key to effective performance here is the processing of feedback information concerning the state of the environment and the selection of subroutines of movement patterns in order to adjust to the changing environment.

No doubt all tennis teachers have seen beginners who could execute a flawless stroke when dropping and hitting the tennis ball, but who could not play a successful game of tennis. Perhaps the wrong objectives were emphasized and reinforced by the grading process. Physical education teachers would do well to classify the types of skills required to correct their emphasis.

FITTS'S LEVELS OF DIFFICULTY

Fitts (1965) recognized the need to develop an adequate task taxonomy. He attempted to classify the tasks according to their degree of difficulty and the processes involved. He also took into account the conditions existing prior to the initiation of a behavior sequence as well as discrete beginnings and endings of a movement pattern.

According to Fitts the task features that can be specified and classified are those dealing with: (1) the degree of body involvement, and (2) the extent of external influences or external pacing. Body involvement was further distinguished by determining if the body was in motion prior to the execution of the critical element in the sport task. Thus, the extent to which an individual was prepared or "set" for action was an important characteristic in his classification system. The external environment was evaluated to determine whether the execution of the task was self-paced or externally paced.

Fitts identified three levels of difficulty for his classification of tasks, labeled I, II, and III. Difficulty was arranged in hierarchical order with level I being the least difficult and level III the most difficult. Briefly, a Level I task is one in which the performer and the object are at rest prior to initiation of action. Level II tasks are those in which one of the two, either performer or object, is moving. Level III involves movement of both the performer and object prior to initiation of the critical element in the movement pattern. A football quarterback throwing a roll-out pass to a moving player is an example of Level III task. Both the performer and the receiver are in motion. The critical element is the release of the ball. A tennis player moving to return a forehand drive is an example of a Level III task; baseball batters perform Level II tasks; and croquet players execute Level I tasks.

LEVEL I TASKS. In these tasks, the body is at rest prior to the beginning of a response sequence, and the movement pattern initiated affects a relatively fixed or stable object. Since the object is not moving in space, the task is self-initiated or self-paced. There are no external requirements to determine when a person will act.

An example is a golfer addressing a golf ball. The ball is stationary and the golfer is stationary before he initiates the action of the swing. There are no external influences (other than the players behind him on the course) to dictate when the swing must be executed.

LEVEL II TASKS. The behavior sequence of these tasks is initiated either while the body is in motion and the external object is fixed, or while the body is stationary and the external object is in motion.

One of the difficulties of the Fitts classification system is the difficulty in identifying the critical element of a skill. For example, is bowling Level I or Level II? If one assumes that the critical element is the release of the ball, then the player is moving prior to release and, since the pins are stationary, it can be classified as Level II. On the other hand, if one assumes that the critical element in bowling is the approach itself, then because the performer is stationary prior to the initiation of the movement pattern and the pins are certainly not moving, bowling becomes Level I difficulty.

Unfortunately, Fitts did not finsh his taxonomy before his death. One can only speculate as to what he had in mind regarding the degree of body involvement. It does seem logical that, since he did state that the degree of body involvement was *prior* to initiation of the movement pattern, we should classify bowling as a Level I task.

Examples of Level II sport tasks are a batter hitting a moving baseball, a skier going through a slalom gate, a baseball catcher catching a pitched ball, and a hunter shooting at a moving bird. In each of these cases it is clear that the object is moving and the body is at rest.

LEVEL III TASKS. In Level III tasks, both the body and the external object are in motion before the particular sequence begins.

A basketball player on the run catching a pass is an example of a Level III task. Similarly, a quarterback in football dropping back to avoid his opponent and simultaneously throwing the ball to a moving receiver is an example of a Level III task. Situations in which one player is evading another usually require the execution of Level III tasks.

While it might seem that this hierarchy of difficulty is misleading (after all hitting a golf ball appears as difficult as hitting a baseball) one can imagine how much more difficult it would be to hit a moving golf ball!

SUMMARY OF FITTS'S TAXONOMY. Fitts based his classification system on the assumption that a man performing a skill is operating as a closed loop feedback system. In such a system, the internal feedback loops are as important as the new information input from the external environment. Information about the response pattern prior to the execution is as important as ongoing information during the performance.

A Level III task requires the person to process internal feedback information concerning his movements at the same time that he processes information about the external objects. Processing internal information while the body is moving is more difficult than when the body is at rest because more information must be decoded. A Level III task is more difficult than a Level I task. Level I tasks do not involve the processing of information regarding moving objects, nor is the body moving prior to the initiation of the sequence pattern. Temporal patterning of objects in the external environment is not required because the objects are not moving in space. This aspect of Fitts's classification system is similar to Knapp's closed skill classification in regard to the factors of spatial/temporal control.

The ideas concerning the relative difficulty of the task is an improvement over the traditional classification system of beginning, intermediate, and advanced. Instead of classifying the level of performance of the player, the difficulty of the movement is identified in relation to the task requirements the performer must accomplish. We should not assume, however, that because a performer is able to execute a task of Level III difficulty he is more skilled than a person who executes a Level II task. Each skill simply calls for a different type of feedback information to be processed.

Fitts's classification system is useful in developing a progression of teaching to be used in learning sport tasks. A player who desires to perform a Level III task may find it helpful to practice the skill first as a Level II task. For example, the beginning basketball player learning to shoot should probably practice first in a stationary position (Level I). He should next progress to moving and then shooting, performing a jump shot or a lay-up (Level II). Then he may practice moving toward the basket, receiving a pass, and shooting (Level III).

AN EXTENSION OF FITTS'S TAXONOMY. Fitts was unable to finish his taxonomy and there are obvious omissions in it. Further work might have resulted in additions that would have answered some of the shortcomings indicated here.

The taxonomy was based on the principle of determining the difficulty of the skill according to the degree of body involvement and the extent of internal and external pacing. Unfortunately, all sport tasks can not be classified clearly in one of his three levels of difficulty. For example, how should the task of hitting a pitched ball that is curving be classified? Catching a spinning frisbee? Where should the task of tackling a ball carrier fit into the classification scheme? In other words, some tasks are more difficult because of the speed, angle, or spin of the moving object. Perhaps another level should be defined for tasks of these kinds. A Level IV task might be identified; or perhaps these tasks should be placed as a subcategory of Level II. The flight, speed, spin, and/or angle of a moving object could then be considered.

Another situation that requires some additional form of classification is the task used in many sports of evading an opponent in order to propel an object to a teammate who also must evade his opponent. This seems to utilize some factors from both Levels II and III.

Other questions simply reinforce the complexity of classifying sport tasks and further emphasize the need to "fill in the gaps." They must be answered if we are to improve our methods of teaching our students. For example, how should we classify situations in which several skills are used one after the other? Is a task that requires the sequential ordering of several individual tasks, or the combining of several complex subroutines, more difficult than the various levels identified above?

VANEK AND CRATTY'S ABILITIES AND GAMES CLASSIFICATION

Vanek and Cratty (1970) presented a classification system based on Kodym's typology. Kodym's typology explored the psychological demands, abilities, and personality traits needed for certain games and sports. Vanek and Cratty divided sporting tasks into five groups: (1) sporting activities involving hand-eye coordination, (2) activities requiring total body coordination, (3) sports requiring total mobilization of body energy, (4) activities in which injury or death are imminent, and (5) sports involving the anticipation of movements of other people. Each category of sport activities demands that the successful individual have certain physical and psychological components or abilities.

The reader will note the term "sporting" tasks instead of "sport" tasks. The word sporting may have been selected deliberately because of the emphasis placed on the personality traits of superior athletes, i.e., contenders in sport.

SPORTING ACTIVITIES REQUIRING HAND-EYE COORDINATION. Activities involving hand-eye coordination include archery, shooting, goal shooting, etc. The performer needs to have a tracking ability or the ability to respond visually to cues from the target. Psychologically these performers are exposed to stress, both external and internal. Stress may be more detrimental near the end of the performance than near the beginning. External stress may be more detrimental than internal stress.

SPORTING ACTIVITIES REQUIRING TOTAL BODY COORDINATION. Sports in which the performer's task is to move his body through space in a pleasing or aesthetic manner involve total body coordination. Diving, water ballet, modern dance, figure skating, and gymnastics are examples of this type of activity. One's body image is of particular importance. There is a great amount of pre-task tension. The ability to balance and to be aware of the location of the body in space are vital for success. In these activities, habits of movement must be established.

SPORTING ACTIVITIES REQUIRING TOTAL MOBILIZATION OF BODY ENERGY. Activities such as distance running, swimming, rowing, and football call for physical power and endurance. Psychologically, these athletes must be able to ignore pain. They must have a high level of determination and a high arousal level to persist in these activities.

A subcategory of this classification includes activities which call for quick explosive mobilization of energy, i.e., shot-putting, sprinting, high jumping, etc.

SPORTING ACTIVITIES IN WHICH INJURY OR DEATH ARE IMMINENT. Race car driving, downhill skiing, and parachute jumping are high risk activities. They call for sound judgment and quick reaction time. Most involve speed and thus demand good control, and self-discipline.

SPORTING ACTIVITIES REQUIRING THE ANTICIPATION OF MOVEMENTS OF OTHER PEOPLE. Team sports call for anticipation of movements of other people. The ability to predict and anticipate are important attributes for success in these sporting activities. Participants generally possess average and above average intelligence and have the ability to utilize past experiences.

Vanek and Cratty listed several subcategories of this group: (1) games using a net (tennis, volleyball, table tennis), (2) games in which direct aggression and personal contact are present (football, soccer), and (3) games involving parallel play or "taking turns" (golf, bowling, baseball). In the first category, no direct aggression is possible and the abilities of attention and agility are important. In games that call for direct aggression, mental and physical toughness as well as speed and endurance are necessary components. Those games in which individuals play concurrently involve no direct aggression. These games demand a high level of tactical strategy, as well as the ability to pace oneself.

SUMMARY OF VANEK AND CRATTY'S CLASSIFICATION SYSTEM. As Vanek and Cratty pointed out, many sporting activities involve a combination of several different classifications. Like the other classification systems presented, there are exceptions. There are always some sports that do not fall completely into one category but rather overlap several categories. Vanek's and Cratty's classification system was presented to lend insight into the various types of personality components needed for high level participation in physical contests. The classification is interesting, although it does not tell us much about learning rate or performance levels.

SUMMARY

In this chapter various types of taxonomies were discussed. Each taxonomy is based upon a principle (or principles) that serve as the guiding factors in the determination of the classification of movements. Each taxonomy attempts to classify tasks to enable the teacher to specify to the learner what the task calls for. The assumption is that the teacher will develop better methods of instruction if he has some understanding of the complex factors involved in various tasks. Developing or selecting a viable taxonomy is the first step to be taken if the instructor desires to improve methods of instruction and enhance learning.

No taxonomy is complete since not all sport tasks can be classified into any one taxonomy. However, it is a beginning. A better understanding of the analysis of sport tasks will aid in the development of methods of instruction, and also in the specification and understanding of research analysis of skill acquisition.

Each taxonomy presented offers a unique way of examining sport tasks. Traditional taxonomies have dealt with the force and extent of movements or the level and number of performers involved. The open-and-closed taxonomy deals with the environmental requirements, the location of important feedback information, and the objective of the skill. Fitts's levels of difficulty consider the condition existing prior to execution and emphasize the importance of self-pacing and external pacing as well as the degree of body involvement. The classification of Vanek and Cratty is useful for defining specific requirements of various sporting games and activities and may aid in explaining why certain people are attracted to various sports.

Since man receives information from various sources (depending upon the type of movement component involved in the task), some classification system is needed to enable physical education teachers to develop reasonable, effective, and logical analyses of sport tasks. Identification of critical components or crucial elements of performance should help teachers simplify the learning process so that greater numbers of students can achieve satisfaction from the attainment of skill.

CHAPTER NINE

THE
INSTRUCTIONAL
PROCESS

The success or failure of the actual methods used by the teacher in an attempt to modify the behavior of the student lies in the course of action. Four steps should be employed in identifying the most appropriate instructional process for each separate teaching situation: (1) assess the entering behavior of the student, (2) analyze the task to be learned, (3) determine the role of the teacher in relation to the instructional procedures, and (4) assess the terminal performance that signifies accomplishment of the task.

The instructional process cannot be based exclusively on the laws of learning. Although broad generalizations about learning have proved useful in understanding the commonalities of the total learning process, the laws of learning do not help the teacher identify and select the exact techniques that are the best for each situation.

The four steps suggested here are one way of analyzing a situation and planning the learning environment. Inexperienced teachers will find the sequence especially helpful in learning to "read" a class, i.e., in assessing the needs of the students and designing an effective program to help students learn skills.

ASSESSING THE ENTERING BEHAVIOR
OF THE STUDENT

To establish an environment in which each student can achieve some success, the teacher must be knowledgeable about what each student brings to the learning situation in terms of desires, capacities, limitations, abilities, and past experiences.

Many teachers begin the development of a unit by identifying the objectives they, the teachers, wish the students to accomplish. Unfortunately, too few teachers make an honest effort to identify student goals or desires, and to adjust their own objectives to make the two compatible. Students who complain that classes "are a waste of time" are often saying that they, the students, seek different outcomes than those being sought by their teachers.

Desirable goals to be achieved through instruction should be identified as *terminal behavior*—the actual performance the student will display at the end of the instructional unit. Reasonable terminal goals cannot be stated until one has determined what the student may wish to accomplish in relation to his initial level of performance.

Many teachers are inclined to set higher goals for students than students set for themselves. On the other hand, many students may seek higher goals than the teacher holds for the class. Other students may seek a level of performance that is unreasonable or unattainable because of the lack of class time or the lack of capabilities in the individual. Anytime there is a discrepancy in the goals being sought, some adjustment must be made.

The assessment of a learner's desires, capacities, and limitations can be accomplished in several ways. Questioning the student about his reasons for wanting to learn a particular task or discussing his ambitions in casual conversation is one means of obtaining insight. Knowledge of capacities and limitations may be determined through the use of various objective tests of skill and knowledge, aptitude or achievement tests, and subjective ratings by the instructor.

Prior experience is extremely important in determining the appropriate starting point for instruction. Every individual entering a learning situation has some experience upon which to draw, some point of reference to use. All persons have processed information before coming to the class. All have had some experience in the subroutines or some part of them, even though the subroutines occurred in different contexts. Where or in what situation the experience occurred is not as important as the fact that it has occurred. Individuals may have learned from TV, private lessons, friends, or relatives. Learning situations are not restricted to organized classes; in fact, some class experiences have hindered learning.

If the instructor is aware of earlier learning experiences, he may be able to utilize common language expressions to call forth "sets" or previous experiences associated with the task. Every beginner has certain responses in his repertoire of behavioral sequences that can aid or hinder the learning of a new task. Awareness of prior learning experiences provide the instructor with information that may assist the learner to master a new task.

For example, instructors in physical education often assume that all their students desire to excel in the specific sport being learned and thus use the experts' standard. Meanwhile, the student may prefer to learn the level of performance required in recreational situations. If a student desires to play "back yard" volleyball instead of competitive volleyball, and the teacher is aware of the desired terminal behavior, the learning situation will be structured so that the learner can accomplish his personal objective first. However, during the early stages of learning, the instructor may try to influence the student to strive for a higher level of achievement, especially if the student is successful with the level he originally set. Self-concept, level of aspiration, and fear of failure must be acknowledged by the instructor as he deals with the student. The good teacher is the one who subtly aids the student to achieve more than he expected to without force.

The main criterion to be used in establishing terminal goals is to state the goals in terms of the observable behavior desired. The teacher, in describing the goals, must communicate to the learner the behavioral sequence he will be performing. The learner will be aided further if terminal goals are stated in terms of an executive plan.

In many cases the executive plan calls for learning *how* to play a game or sport as well as learning the individual skills within the sport. All games can be analyzed by dividing them into three phases: (1) the skills or movement patterns involved in the game, (2) the offensive and defensive moves, and (3) the rules controlling the use of the skills and strategies.

The first phase must be determined by the student's terminal goals or objectives. What does the student wish to accomplish? Is he desirous of highly competitive play, or back yard recreational play? The teacher must be aware of the student's goal before he can structure the learning situation.

It seems safe to assume that most students would rather "play" the game as quickly as possible than try to master all the various skills. Unfortunately, many teachers do not recognize this desire and insist that students learn the skills through the use of drill formations before they can play the game. If the teacher agrees that students should become involved in the game situation as soon as possible, then he must determine the necessary movement patterns and skills necessary to this end. For example, in order to play volleyball the only skill a player needs is the volley. The game can be modified so that it can be started with a volley.

Strategies and skills should be taught simultaneously. All strategies can be divided into offensive and defensive actions. An offensive action involves capitalizing on space left free by an opponent and/or maneuvering to open a space. Defensive action calls for players to avoid leaving open spaces or areas. Thus, in volleyball the volley must be taught in conjunction with ball placement, defensive floor coverage, backing up players, change of direction, and deceptive tactics. There are beginning strategies to be taught with beginning skills, intermediate strategies to be accomplished with intermediate skills, and advanced strategies to be learned with advanced skills. Waiting until all the skills have been accomplished before teaching the strategies is an inefficient way of teaching.

The rules of the game should be introduced as the players become sufficiently acquainted with the game and learn the implications of the offensive and defensive actions. Teaching rules on a "rainy day" or saving them until the last week of a unit may cloud the student's association between rules, skills, and strategy.

Further discussion of what to teach will be presented under the next step, analyzing the task. Obviously, task analysis must consider the purposes and desires of the students.

ANALYZING THE TASK

The ability to analyze the task confronting a student is probably the most crucial step in the sequence of determining a method of instruction. Task analysis begins with a classification of the skills to be acquired, i.e., the establishment of an appropriate task taxonomy. The task taxonomy will aid the teacher in identifying the critical components of a task in relation to the objectives or desires indicated by the student.

Ideally, individuals preparing to teach would develop one or more classification systems as undergraduates. They could identify the critical components in the execution of tasks in relation to the objectives they, themselves, seek in performance. They modify the task analysis in relation to the objectives or desires indicated by their students.

Task analysis involves two things: (1) a classification of skills in a taxonomy, and (2) the analysis of the critical components of a task. Each involves a procedural thought process which the teacher accomplishes *prior to* beginning the actual instruction period. Although the general principles or criteria used were discussed in chapter 8, the procedure to be used in employing the principles is demonstrated in the following pages.

A CLASSIFICATION SYSTEM

Can the task be classified in one taxonomy or are several taxonomies appropriate? A single taxonomy is seldom suitable for all skills. A combination of several factors from different taxonomies may be the most appropriate.

Table 1, presents a sample classification system of selected sport skills which may help the reader understand the process of task analysis. Tasks are first classified as to whether they are open or closed. (The reader will recall that an open task involves temporal/spatial control of the environment and a closed task involves spatial regulation.) Thus, archery target shooting is a closed task while skeet shooting is an open task. In archery, the target is not moving and thus one must regulate the spatial qualities; in skeet shooting, the target is moving—spatial control and timing are needed in order to accomplish the task.

Similarly a task can be analyzed to determine whether or not movements are externally or self-paced. An externally paced movement requires the performer to anticipate. A self-paced task calls for individual determination of initiation of movement.

The task can be further analyzed by determining the state of the system prior to movement. Is the object at rest? Is the person at rest? Are both moving? Other questions to be answered involve type of movement, main feedback sources, and objective of the task.

Answering these questions helps the teacher examine the actual requirements of the task. This process, in turn, points out various *critical* sources of feedback. For example, processing internal feedback is important in closed skills where body transport is involved (e.g., a gymnastic event). Object manipulation calls for external feedback processing as do tasks involving awareness of other teammates. Race car driving demands the processing of information regarding the action of the car itself.

It should be noted that the suggested classification system shown in Table 1 lists critical elements of the task which demand certain attention. It does not imply that the ones checked are the *only* critical elements involved. For example, intrinsic (task) feedback is the critical information to process under race car driving but this does not imply that it is the only source of feedback. Feedback information is received from several sources.

In Table 1 specific movement patterns were selected for analysis. One can also approach classification of movement by analyzing the specific patterns used within a game situation. Table 2, for example,

TABLE 1. A Suggested Classification System for Selected Sports

Classification	Archery Target Shooting	Sheet Shooting	Gymnastic Vault	Sports Track-Race 50 Yard Dash	Bowling	Tennis Forehand Drive	Race Car Driving
Type of Environmental Regulation							
Closed (Spatial Control)	X		X	X	X		
Open (Temporal/Spatial Control)		X				X	X
Pacing of Movements							
Externally Paced		X				X	X
Self-Paced	X		X	X	X		
State of System Prior to Movement							
Object and Body at Rest	X		X	X	X		
One of the Two Moving		X				X	
Both Moving							X
Type of Movement							
Postural-Stability	X	X					
Transport							
Limb					X	X	
Body			X	X	X	X	
Object Manipulation	X	X					X
Main Feedback Sources							
Internal	X	X	X	X	X	X	
External	X	X			X	X	
Intrinsic (Task)							X
Objective							
Judge's Rating of Form			X				
Points Scored	X	X			X	X	
Speed (Time)				X			X

TABLE 2. A CLASSIFICATION SYSTEM OF SELECTED MOVEMENTS INVOLVED IN BASKETBALL

Classification	Free Throw	Movement Patterns		
		Shooting During the Game	Passing to a Stationary Player	Passing to Moving Player
Type of Environmental Regulation				
Closed (Spatial Control)	X			
Open (Temporal/Spatial Control)		X	X	X
Pacing of Movements				
Externally Paced		X	X	X
Self-Paced	X			
State of System Prior to Movement				
Object and Body at Rest	X	X	X	
One of the Two Moving				X
Both Moving				
Type of Movement				
Postural-Stability	X			
Transport				
Limb	X	X	X	X
Body				
Object Manipulation	X	X	X	X
Main Feedback Sources				
Internal	X			
External	X	X	X	X
Instrinsic (Task)				
Objective				
Judge's Rating Form				
Points Scored	X	X	X	X
Speed (Time)				

presents a selected group of movement patterns used in basketball. The free throw situation in basketball involves closed skills, self-pacing, Level I difficulty, postural and limb movement, and internal and external feedback processing. But the situation changes when shooting a basket during a game or passing to another player. The reader is encouraged to add other skills to this chart or to analyze a specific sport task.

ANALYSIS OF CRITICAL COMPONENTS

Task analysis is based on the assumption that any task can be analyzed into a set of component tasks which are quite distinct from each other in terms of the operations needed to produce an effective performance.

The components of the task are the subroutines involved in the total performance. Once the components have been determined, the teacher should decide which are the *critical* components of the task, that is, identify those that are the most difficult or crucial parts of the task. They may be subroutines which, in the experience of the instructor, students have the most difficulty in mastering. The most crucial subroutine may be one that is central to the objective of the student, or the most influential in its effect on other subroutines.

The subroutines considered critical are those that must receive concentrated effort if the learner is to accomplish his executive plan. The reader is reminded here that past experiences (already established routines) will vary from student to student. The age and comprehension ability of the learner will influence the identification of critical components, also.

At this point, the instructor must consider such questions as: What automatic subroutines will need to be modified? What subroutines should become automatic? How can practice conditions be arranged to optimize conditions so that each of the critical components of the task can be achieved by the learner? Are there some subroutines to which another subroutine needs to be added in order to compensate for an already automatic subroutine?

When these questions have been answered, the next procedure is the organization of the learning situation in such a way that each of the critical components will insure optimal mediational effects from one subroutine to another. Thus, not only the sequential organization of the subroutines must be considered, but also the temporal patterning or time interval between components.

SAMPLE TASK ANALYSIS: BEGINNING BOWLING. In order to aid the reader in understanding the procedural thought process encountered in task analysis the following example is presented:

The task of beginning bowling can be divided into three subroutines. These are: (1) the approach, (2) moving the ball, and (3) the release of the ball. Further examination of each subroutine reveals that the approach consists of steps that get progressively longer and faster and end with a slide. Since this is not the way a person normally walks, the subroutine of walking will have to be modified. *Conscious* effort and practice will be needed to overcome his habitual walking pattern.

The second subroutine involved in the task of bowling is moving a ball through space. Although the performer is accustomed to swinging his arm, he is not familiar with moving a ball that weighs between twelve and sixteen pounds.

The third subroutine involves the release of the ball. A smooth release is characterized by a roll of the ball rather than a drop or throw. Thus the beginner must learn to bend his left knee (assuming he is right-handed) and release the ball smoothly on the lane, not on the approach area. The ball should land on the lane like an airplane landing on a runway.

Once the subroutines are determined, the teacher must decide how the learner can best master each subroutine. Elements within each subroutine must be examined to determine those that are critical. Critical elements refer to those components that ensure successful accomplishment of the performance; their absence implies failure. The beginner may or may not be able to perform all subroutines.

The decision of which critical element to stress can be accomplished by possible outcomes in regard to each subroutine. For example, what are the possible outcomes in the subroutines involved in bowling? Some students may relegate the approach to the lower level of control (not consciously think about it) and the result will be a normal walk, i.e., they will not take progressively longer and faster steps. Concentrating on arm swing and moving of the ball may be effective, but the "normal walk" approach may render subroutines two and three ineffective.

Other students may concentrate on the approach and relegate the arm swing to the lower levels of control. They will end up "holding" the ball during the approach or swinging it late. If they fail to start the ball moving they will either drop it or rush the arm swing.

In order to be effective in accomplishing all three subroutines, a student must concentrate on the critical elements within each subroutine. We know that man is supposedly a single channel system. How, then, can students learn to deal with several subroutines at once? The answer is that the students must learn to "time share." They must learn to deal with critical elements in one subroutine and then critical elements in another subroutine, etc. They must learn to shift their level of concentration.

Once again, the task of beginning bowling will be used to further explain the idea of time sharing. The critical component in the first subroutine (approach) is a *short* first step coordinated with the arm swing. If one uses a four-step approach, there must be four phases in the arm swing. The space covered by the distance the ball travels on the first step must be longer than the first step itself if the feet and the ball are to be synchronized for a proper release. The "time sharing" student must think of starting the ball in motion *before* taking his first step of the approach. Thus, the cue "push away the ball, *then* start the approach" must be internalized by the student.

The student must concentrate first on moving the ball and then on taking a short first step. The critical component in the push-away is in directing the ball toward the pins. Practicing these sequential acts before completing the entire approach can be very helpful in aiding the student to time share. This might be termed "part" practice. In this case, however, a part of the task is being practiced *after* the task analysis has been accomplished, not because a generalization has been made that part practice helps acquire skill. Part practice is beneficial in the above example because it forces the student to learn the correct start of the sequential movement. As the reader will recall, starting correctly is extremely important in all sequential movement.

Once the beginner learns this and it becomes automatic he is ready to proceed to mastering the third subroutine (the release).

Until now nothing has been mentioned regarding the second and third steps of the approach (assuming a four-step approach). Providing information regarding the action of the arm and feet during this part of the approach is not necessary because the performer is moving too quickly and he cannot consciously process information or time share. If he tries to do this it will be quite obvious and he will make a very slow, deliberate approach. He actually then, must be told to preprogram his approach. He must learn the start of the approach (short first step and push away) and "think" about the sequential movement *before* the movement is started.

The critical element involved in the third subroutine is bending the left knee and releasing the ball beyond the foul line or on the lane itself. Practice on this subroutine can be accomplished by approaching the foul line and taking a one step approach. The beginner should concentrate on rolling the ball with a smooth release. Once this has become automatic the student is ready to begin the entire approach.

Thus far our attention has been directed to the student who is learning to perform a task. Suppose, after assessing the behavior brought to the situation, the teacher realizes that the students are not beginners at all. Suppose the students are experienced, have several established subroutines, but also some errors of execution. Task analysis is still extremely important; however, now its use should vary, at least slightly. Woe to the teacher who begins at the beginning again under the faulty assumption that the errors will be corrected best by starting over.

THE NEED FOR TASK ANALYSIS. Unfortunately, many beginning teachers lack the ability to start teaching in a variety of ways or at different places in a progression. Some are inclined to "teach as they were taught" and disregard the information gained in assessing the behavior of their students. Others will teach the sequence presented in a techniques book; i.e., they disregard individuals of the class and use the specified progression as a "crutch" for teaching all classes.

The teacher who has developed a taxonomy of tasks or a classification of skills, will have a head start for helping more advanced students and experienced performers with error problems. A classification system that applies to several sports can be like a regional map to a tourist who is traveling through several states. The teacher has a guide to follow and can be looking for clues to the next step.

The good classification system will enable the teacher to start a teaching plan in different places because similarities among skills will be evident. It has been said there is commonality in all movement patterns, only the purposes (and therefore the details) vary. Teachers of physical education should learn to recognize similarities and interrelationships in movement patterns as aids to their students. Why teach each sport as though it were different from all other sports?

Task analysis can help in other situations, also. It will aid in teaching a physical education class that includes beginners and a wide variety of experienced players, including a few who may be highly skilled. Obviously the beginners must start by learning basic skills, but must the experienced students repeat the beginning skills, too? If the task is a closed skill, self-paced, or relies primarily on internal feedback, students can be given different tasks independent of each other. If the tasks being learned are open tasks, externally paced, or reliant on external feedback, some unique approach to the teaching situation is necessary.

Earlier it was suggested that student goals must be considered in task analysis. If the situation calls for a unique approach because student experience and goals are extremely diversified, careful task analysis can help teachers select what might be termed "common denominator skills." It may be possible to select skills the experienced players do least well to combine with basic skills beginners should learn. An example taken from actual experience will illustrate the point.

A basketball class for college women included players who had played in interscholastic competition, some of whom had been on state championship teams or had been selected as all-state players. It also included beginners whose sole experience had been cheering the play as spectators, and various degrees in between. The beginners wanted to learn to play the game well enough to play with the experienced players; the top players wanted to play rather than drill. The question was what to do to provide a satisfying learning situation for all types of players.

The instructor's analysis of the players' capabilities in relation to the various student goals indicated a need for something definite and sequential for the beginners, and yet somewhat new to the experienced players—in this case, a system of play that could serve as an equalizer. The beginners were taught a specific type of shifting zone defense and were successful against skilled players whose experience had been limited to player-to-player defense.

Another example from basketball will illustrate a different approach used when the situation indicated a need for a common denominator. In an average girls' basketball class the scoring capabilities are usually very limited. Although the experienced players will not respond to analysis and drill of shooting techniques, the beginners need practice on these skills that will enable them to score. Interestingly enough, analysis showed the greatest need to be for evasive tactics rather than shooting skills. Players were unable to free themselves for open shots and scored poorly because they were shooting off balance, too hurriedly, etc. The common denominator in this case was instruction in basic evasive tactics of feinting, pivoting, cutting inside an opponent, plus combinations involving teammates screening and picking off opponents.

Experience in handling a variety of teaching situations is of great value only if the teacher consciously tries new approaches with each class. Conscientious exploration to search out the best ways to enhance learning will provide students with better opportunities for skill learning. No amount of experience will help the teacher who is satisfied to teach every class the same way and who prefers several classes in the same subject on the assumption that only one preparation need be made per day. Every class is different; every class must first be assessed and then taught in relation to the task analysis.

THE ROLE OF THE TEACHER

Many schools devote a great deal of time to curriculum revision. However, little has been done to change the actual teaching process. Perhaps the reason is that the most difficult component in the teaching system to modify is the individual teacher. The difficulty may lie in the fact that the role of the teacher has not been clarified. Is the role of the teacher that of a disciplinarian? A provider of knowledge? A motivator? A friend? A threat? Before sound learning environments can be structured, the teacher's role must be defined.

The teacher actually plays several roles at different times depending on the situation. There are four main roles the teacher may use in relation to information gained from the entering behavior of the student, and analyzing the task: (1) aiding the student to code information, (2) determining the mode of practice, (3) designing the training media, and (4) providing feedback. Each is important at different times for different students. The roles are not listed in any priority order because a teacher may use one with one student and another with another student within the same period.

To be successful in accomplishing any of the roles, rapport between the student and teacher must be established. The establishment of rapport implies that meaningful communication is carried on between the student and the teacher. When rapport is established, the student's goals are taken into consideration and the teacher is aware of the student as an individual. In other words, mutual respect and a give and take relationship have been established.

Students vary as do teachers. They vary in ability to communicate as well as in ability to perform. Each class, even those selected on the basis of homogeneity, will demonstrate a range of ability. Teachers must begin where the students are, or where the majority is, in performance level. To begin at a higher level is discouraging for the student. To begin at a lower level is redundant and leads to boredom and discipline problems. The ability to assess performance levels and/or "read" a class becomes crucial in establishing rapport with the class as a whole.

ENCODING INFORMATION

Encoding means the processing of input information. The reader will recall that information is processed by transforming words, concepts, and ideas into symbols. Some information will be relegated by the learner to the storage system; other types of information will be filtered out or disregarded. The teacher must help the student select information to be encoded, and also aid the student in the encoding by: (1) asking questions, (2) pulling together major points of emphasis, (3) linking old and new knowledge, and (4) pointing out important cues to attend to.

TYPES OF INFORMATION. Posner (1964) demonstrated through experimentation that man processes information in three ways: (1) conservation, (2) reduction, and (3) creation. The fundamental assumption of Posner's classification is that man is a transmitter of information. The basic consideration is the relationship of the output to the input. In other words, what type of information is man asked to process? Must man conserve, reduce, or create information?

INFORMATION CONSERVATION. In a task requiring the conservation of information, the subject's output must utilize all the information in the input; i.e., the output must be equal to the input. Because information is reproduced, the term conservation is used. If the information output is reduced or less than the input, it is termed an error. Rote learning or memorization is an example of an information conservation task. In this case the information output is identical to the information input. Physical educators too often have expected this type of performance when students are tested on information dispensed during a rainy day chalk talk.

In most instances, demonstrations of sport skills can be classified as information conservation tasks. This is particularly true if the student is to imitate or mimic the demonstrator. The student must process and conserve all the information from the input system. Quite obviously it is difficult to have an errorless performance. It is especially difficult and virtually impossible to have an errorless performance if the task is complex or if speed of processing is important. For this reason, the demonstration may be slowed down or repeated several times in an effort to help the student process all the information successfully and then execute a conservation type output.

If the task requires students to produce what has been demonstrated, precision will depend upon (1) the compatibility or congruence of the relationship between the input and output, and (2) the student's ability to discriminate important inputs to be reproduced. This aspect of information theory affords some explanation as to why beginning learners have so much difficulty executing what they have seen demonstrated.

INFORMATION REDUCTION. In a second task of Posner's classification system, man must reduce the amount of information provided by the input and produce an output that is a condensation of the input. This type of task is termed an *information reduction task*. Examples of such types of tasks are condensing a book, writing an abstract, or refereeing a ball game. In all cases man filters out some information from the input and reduces the extent of the output. A referee of a ball game is performing a reduction type task when he takes in all the relevant stimuli, reduces or filters out irrelevant information, and renders a decision based on stimuli important to his task. His output is the result of this process. In order to filter out information relevant to the task he must have a standard with which to compare incoming stimuli. If an error in a game is quite noticeable, the job of information reduction is easier. If, however, information is presented at a high rate of speed (i.e., much information is given out in a short period of time) the task is more difficult. When the official is familiar with what he is to look for in the game, his task is much easier. Likewise, once the official knows the rules and understands what information is necessary for a decision, the task becomes easier.

Other types of tasks that involve reduction are those involving condensation of information. In the case of writing an abstract, the author must take in more information than he needs for the abstract, or output. Logically, the more information one needs to reduce, or the more complex the information, the longer the time generally required to complete the process. In tasks that call for a condensation of information, it is extremely important that only *irrelevant* information be omitted, not *relevant* information. Omitting an important point in an abstract can change the entire meaning and idea of the original work. Omissions of this type often occur when material is lifted out of context.

A coach who receives a scouting report must process all the information concerning the strategy of the opponents, reduce this information, and synthesize it into meaningful capsules for his players. A football coach must decide which plays and what variations need to be mastered by his team in order for them to be "ready" for the opponents. Thus, scouting and subsequent game planning are forms of information reduction tasks.

INFORMATION CREATION. Probably the most difficult tasks in Posner's classification system are those labeled information creation tasks. These are tasks in which the output is an elaboration of the input—the output is *more* than the input. This type of task is executed when the student learns to rearrange, reorder, or create new information as opposed to reproducing or condensing input.

Examples of this type of task are a dancer creating a dance, a gymnast devising a routine, a swimmer planning a synchronized routine, or a scout of a basketball game condensing the offensive and defensive plays of the opponents and also suggesting a strategy to use against them. In creation type tasks, the performer must utilize all the input and either elaborate, extend, or rearrange it.

MODE OF PRACTICE AND TRAINING MEDIA

Selection of the mode of practice depends upon the task classification as well as the knowledge of the individuals in the group. Questions involved in selecting the mode of practice are: Should the process of self-instruction be employed? Should one emphasize movement patterns of a stereotyped or of an anticipatory flexible nature? Should there be practice on certain subroutines or on the entire executive program?

GAME SIMULATION. Simulation is one type of practice which is frequently employed in teaching sport tasks. Simulation involves making a situation as similar as possible to the actual situation. The advantage in a simulated situation is that the instructor can often control and/or manipulate some variables while holding other variables constant.

For example, a basketball instructor can set up certain situations which are similar to a real game. In teaching offensive action, he may manipulate the guards so that the offensive team can see the spatial relationship and the movements of his teammates. First the guards remain stationary while the offensive team maneuvers the ball toward the basket. Then the guards may be allowed to move only their arms while keeping their feet stationary. Finally the guards are allowed to move in relation to the ball. Thus, the forwards experience a situation which becomes more and more like the game—a game simulation that aids them to progressively learn the offensive action.

Frequently physical educators have sought to simulate game situations in drills. Observation of some drill situations leads one to question whether or not the drill was selected on the basis of task analysis. For example, a favorite drill situation used by instructors of team games, e.g., soccer, divides the class into groups of two, each group with a ball. Two players pass the ball back and forth and work on various movement patterns. Does this type of drill actually simulate the game situation? In reality, no! Soccer has twenty-two players and one ball. The teacher may well wonder why, when put into a game, everyone converges on the ball. The answer is, of course, that the drill has emphasized ball play.

Perhaps a better simulated game situation would have the field divided into miniature game situations. The situation of four on four, or two on three would be much more helpful for players to learn to anticipate movements and thus intercept passes. The drill of twosomes passing back and forth is actually a one on one situation. A one on two situation would not be much better because the critical component in soccer is learning how to either force a pass or intercept a pass. With a one on two situation it is obvious that the pass must go to the other person. No learning of anticipation is possible.

FILMS. Another form of training media often employed in learning movement tasks is films. These must be selected in accordance with the analysis of the task and previous knowledge of the student. Is some cases, for example, skills that have been classified as closed are more easily learned through repeated showings of films or film strips. On the other hand, skills that are classified as open would be more satisfactorily taught by use of simulation or viewing game-like situations.

Using films only on rainy days is deplorable. Students are more inclined to think of films as entertainment than as devices to supplement learning. Unfortunately good teaching films are not always readily available. With the increased study of educational technology perhaps this situation will be improved.

PROVIDING FEEDBACK

The teacher also provides feedback to students. As previously mentioned, feedback is much more than knowledge of results. The feedback loop that plays the more important role in learning a specific movement pattern must be determined through task analysis. In some tasks the internal loops play the more important role, and in others, the external stimuli are more valuable.

Meaningful feedback can be obtained and processed if the instructor knows which feedback loops are operating and what types, modes, and methods are available to the teacher and student.

Feedback can be concurrent or terminal. It can evaluate, compare, prescribe, or affect performance. It is extremely important for the instructor to recall the three roles that feedback can play. It can serve to motivate, to reinforce, and to change performance. Feedback can give information about an entire movement sequence, a subroutine, an executive program, a temporal error, or a sequential error.

Feedback is processed by the individual *if* the individual is able to apply the *transformation rule*. According to Annett (1969), a transformation rule is the knowledge of how output is converted into appropriate control action. Thus, the function of the teacher is to provide experiences whereby the learner can discover his own transformation rules. Since skill learning is extremely complex, there may be several transformation rules and the teacher who is least successful may be the one who has only *one* way of doing things. The student may learn to do what the teacher says rather than learning or becoming more familiar with his own functional system and his own transformation rules. No matter what variables one controls, or what the desires of the teacher are, or what reward and punishment systems are used, the student himself is the one who must select the information to process. The teacher can only help the student learn the transformation rule. Thus the old adage: "You can send a boy to school but you cannot make him learn!"

ASSESSING TERMINAL PERFORMANCE

The last step in the instructional process is that of assessing the accomplishment of the task in relation to the specified terminal behavior. Perhaps, the reader can now understand the importance of following all the steps in the instructional process. If the terminal behavior has not been adequately established and communicated to the learner, the student does not have a performance standard by which to evaluate his progress. If the capacities and limitations of the student have not been determined, and are not taken into consideration, the value of past experience cannot be realized, and the amount of progress cannot be identified. If the task is not analyzed, the teacher cannot structure the learning environment. The degree to which the task has been achieved (assessment) must be assessed in relation to the previous action and thought in the first three steps.

Terminal behavior is defined as that which the student does to demonstrate that he has achieved the task. Many physical education tasks can be indicated in terms of measured units; other sports tasks must be evaluated as to the quality of movement performed. In either case, it is generally possible to indicate the minimum level of performance that is satisfactory.

Physical educators often assess terminal performance of students in relation to the performance of champions or top-notch players. This type of assessment is unfair to the average student, no matter how many years he may have been exposed to the activity.

Furthermore, the assessment should be in relation to learning rather than to mere improvement in performance. The reader is reminded of the need to distinguish between learning and performance, and teachers should be aware of those factors that can result in improved performance without learning having taken place.

Students have a right to criticize instructors who assess terminal performance (especially if a grade is involved in the process) if those instructors have not identified the terminal behavior desired, if they use performance and learning as though they were synonymous, if they credit improvement as the major factor in the final assessment, or if they use only standardized skill tests to evaluate performance. Teachers must consider the means by which they make assessments. Age of students, amount of practice, years of experience, length of the instructional period, and other factors must be taken into account when terminal behaviors are identified. The same factors must be considered in the final assessment.

SUMMARY

In some cases, it appears, one learns to teach only when one actually begins to teach. Experience is the best means for aiding teachers. There is no question concerning the value of experience in determining appropriate methods of instruction. However, just as in learning a skill, practice alone isn't the answer. Practice must be accompanied by appropriate feedback.

Many educators advocate knowledge of principles of learning for aiding one to develop appropriate teaching methods. However, principles of learning are not automatically helpful for developing methods to short-cut the learning process.

If it is true that many teachers teach as they were taught, then a model must be presented so that future teachers may learn correct ways of teaching. This statement assumes that the future teacher will be teaching the same kinds of individuals as the model teacher taught. This assumption weakens the statement which does not allow for differences in situations and individuals.

The premise in this chapter is that there are procedures that will enable teachers to better select appropriate methods of instruction. Methods of instruction can be determined by going through a specific process. The process suggested here is to examine the interactions between the teacher, the task, and the students. Teachers have certain habits that can help or hinder the acquisition of a task. Tasks have certain critical components that must be analyzed and examined. Individuals vary in their capacities and limitations as well as in their goals and desires.

Looking at man as a transmitter of information holds great promise for future design of research studies and aids in understanding the different types of tasks man is asked to perform. This type of classification allows for a quantitative description of the task in terms of input measures, central processing requirements, and motor outputs. The type and amount of input and the demands made on the encoding, decoding system and memory storage system can be specified. Perhaps man's decision mechanism could be better understood if exact tasks were delineated.

Although this type of classification system provides great research possibilities, it also gives practicing teachers an opportunity to better understand the type of tasks they are trying to help students accomplish.

If we accept the fact that individuals learn differently, process information differently, react differently, and have different transformation rules, then it follows that students will react differently to the same methods of instruction. Also, teachers are different and they, too, have different results using the same methods. The major problem in developing the instructional plan is putting the student and teacher together.

In order to develop an instructional plan the teacher and the student must be able to communicate. A certain amount of rapport must be established. The teacher's role is varied, but he must develop techniques for "reading" the class and understanding individuals in the group. He must also be able to analyze the task to be learned and define terminal goals and performance objectives.

Once the major considerations of task analysis and individual differences have been systematized, the teacher helps the student code information, designs training media and practice sessions, provides feedback, and assesses performance.

In this chapter, the role of the teacher was likened to that of an orchestra director rather than that of a general dictating to the troops. The teacher directs the learning process and thus aids each individual to become a self-actualizing, self-sufficient individual capable of performing movement to regulate and control his environment.

APPENDIXES
AND
BIBLIOGRAPHY

APPENDIX A: TAXONOMY

The cognitive and affective taxonomy as stated by D. R. Krathwohl, B. S. Bloom, and B. B. Masia, *Taxonomy of Education Objectives* (New York: David McKay Co., Inc., 1964), pp. 49–50.

A summary of a tentative System of Taxonomy of Educational Objectives, Psychomotor Domain, as stated by Elizabeth Jane Simpson, "The Classification of Educational Objectives," *Illinois Teacher of Home Economics*, 10, No. 4 (Winter 1966–67), 135–40.

Psycho-motor

1.0 *Perception*—This is an essential first step in performing a motor act. It is the process of becoming aware of objects, qualities, or relations by way of the sense organs. It is the central portion of the situation-interpretation-action chain leading to purposeful motor activity.

The category of perception has been divided into three subcategories indicating three different levels with respect to the perception process. It seems to the investigator that this level is a parallel of the first category, receiving or attending, in the affective domain.

1.1 *SENSORY STIMULATION*—Impingement of a stimulus (i) upon one or more of the sense organs.

1.2 *CUE SELECTION*—Deciding to what cues one must respond in order to satisfy the particular requirements of task performance.

1.3 *TRANSLATION*—Relating of perception to action in performing a motor act. This is the mental process of determining the meaning of the cues received for action. It involves symbolic translation, that is, having an image or being reminded of something, "having an idea," as a result of cues received. It may involve insight which is essential

Cognitive

1. The cognitive continuum begins with the student's recall and recognition of KNOWLEDGE (1.0);

Affective

1. The affective continuum begins with the student's merely RECEIVING (1.0) stimuli and passively attending to it. It extends through his more actively attending to it,

156

2. it extends through his Comprehension (2.0) of the knowledge,

2. his Responding (2.0) to stimuli on request, willingly responding to these stimuli; and taking satisfaction in this responding,

3. his skill in APPLICATION (3.0) of the knowledge that he comprehends,

3. his VALUING (3.0) the phenomenon or activity so that he voluntarily responds and seeks out ways to respond,

in solving a problem through perceiving the relationships essential to solution. Sensory translation is an aspect of this level. It involves "feedback," that is, knowledge of the effects of the process; translation is a continuous part of the motor act being performed.

2.0 *Set*—Set is a preparatory adjustment or readiness for a particular kind of action or experience.

2.1 *MENTAL SET*—Readiness, in the mental sense, to perform a certain motor act. This involves, as prerequisite, the level of perception and its subcategories which have already been identifed. Discrimination, that is, using judgment in making distinctions is an aspect.

2.2 *PHYSICAL SET*—Readiness in the sense of having made the anatomical adjustments necessary for a motor act to be performed. Readiness, in the physical sense, involves receptor set, that is, sensory attending, or forcusing the attention of the needed sensory organs and postural set, or positioning of the body.

2.3 *EMOTIONAL SET*—Readiness in terms of attitudes favorable to the motor act's taking place. Willingness to respond is implied.

3.0 *Guided response*—This is an early step in the development of skill. Emphasis here is upon the abilities which are components of the more complex skill. Guided response is the overt behavioral act of an individual under the guidance of the instructor. Prerequisite to performance of the act are readiness to respond, in terms of set to produce the overt behavioral act and selection of the appropriate response. Selection of response may be defined as deciding what response must be made in order to satisfy the particular requirements of task performance. There appear to be two major subcategories, imitation and trial and error.

3.1 *IMITATION*—Imitation is the execution of an act as a direct response to the perception of another person performing the act.

APPENDIX A—CONT.

3.2 *TRIAL AND ERROR*—Trying various responses, usually with some rationale for each response, until an appropriate response is achieved. The appropriate response is one which meets the requirements of task performance, that is, "gets the job done" or does it more efficiently. This level may be defined as multiple-response learning in which the proper response is selected out of varied behavior, possibly through the influence of reward and punishment.

4.0 *Mechanism*—Learned response has become habitual. At this level, the learner has achieved a certain confidence and degree of skill in the performance of the act. The act is a part of his repertoire of possible responses to stimuli and the demands of situations where the response is an appropriate one. The response may be more complex than at the preceding level; it may involve some patterning of response in carrying out the task. That is, abilities are combined in action of a skill nature.

5.0 *Complex overt response*—At this level, the individual can perform a motor act that is considered complex because of the movement pattern required. At this level, a high degree of skill has been attained. The act can be carried out smoothly and efficiently, that is, with minimum expenditure of time and energy. There are two subcategories: resolution of uncertainty and automatic performance.

5.1 *RESOLUTION OF UNCERTAINTY*—The act is performed without hesitation of the individual to get a mental picture of task sequence. That is, he knows the sequence required and so proceeds with confidence. The act is here defined as complex in nature.

5.2 *AUTOMATIC PERFORMANCE*—At this level, the individual can perform a finely coordinated motor skill with a great deal of ease and muscle control.

4. his CONCEPTUALIZATION (4.1) of each value responded to,

4. his skill in ANALYSIS (4.0) of situations involving this knowledge, his skill in Synthesis (5.0) of this knowledge into new organizations,.

5. his skill in EVALUATION (6.0) in that area of knowledge to judge the value of material and methods for given purposes.

5. his ORGANIZATION (4.2) of these values into systems and finally organizing the value complex into a single whole, a CHARACTERIZATION (5.0) of the individual.

APPENDIX B:
DISCUSSION QUESTIONS

DISCUSSION QUESTIONS—COGNITIVE KNOWLEDGE

The following are suggested questions for class discussion, review, or examinations. They can also serve as a self-testing device for students.

1. What are the mechanisms involved in executing a skilled act?
2. List variables that affect performance and cause a temporary change in behavior.
3. What has recent research concluded about the plateau of learning?
4. Explain transfer from the viewpoints of associationist and cognitive learning theorists.
5. What principle research finding would support the use of red tennis balls as opposed to white?
6. Does man's ability to use prior information always improve performance?
7. List the characteristics of an executive program.
8. What happens when an adult learns a new skill?
9. What are habits?
10. Define perception, perceptual-motor, sensory-motor.
11. What is the fundamental building block or behavioral unit according to association theory, to cognitive theory, and to cybernetic theory?
12. What are the differences between affective, effective, and cognitive learning?
13. Give examples of information reducing, conserving, and creation tasks.
14. What variables affect reaction time? Movement time?
15. What is attention? What affects what one pays attention to?
16. Match the following terms to the most fitting description:

    a. Augmented feedback   1. Information that is inherent in the task and a result of a person's own actions.

    b. Reinforcing feedback   2. Ongoing information is given.

    c. Concurrent feedback   3. Feedback that appears to affect performance rather than learning.

    d. Regulating feedback (action feedback)   4. Proprioceptive feedback.

    e. Intrinsic feedback   5. The use of manual guidance.

    f. Terminal feedback   6. Demonstrations by an instructor.

    g. None of the above   7. A grade in a course.

17. What is the doctrine of prior entry?
18. Explain negative transfer, positive transfer, proactive inhibition, retroactive inhibition.
19. Discuss and explain retention theories.

20. Define ability.
21. What is executive monitoring, time sharing?
22. What purposes do taxonomies serve?
23. What does the concept of hierarchical organization imply?
24. Define the phenomena of reminiscence.
25. List the important points to be considered in the various phases of learning a skill.

DISCUSSION QUESTIONS—AFFECTIVE KNOWLEDGE

1. What do you consider to be the greatest difficulty to overcome in the area of skill learning before teachers of physical education can improve their methods of teaching?
2. How has or has not your perception of the dynamics of skill acquisition changed as a result of reading this book?
3. Discuss the meaningfulness of learning a skill if you define skill as the accomplishment of an objective as opposed to excellency in movement.
4. Discuss the pros and cons of the following statement: "The description of man as an information processing system implies a mechanistic rather than humanistic viewpoint."

DISCUSSION QUESTIONS—APPLICATION

1. Design and carry out an experiment on any one of the following topics:
   a. Variables affecting reaction time
   b. Variables affecting movement time
   c. Distribution of practice
   d. Retention
   e. Stress
   f. Deprivation of feedback
2. Read the following description written by a person learning to do a left-handed lay-up shot in basketball. She is right-handed, college age, and fairly well-skilled. Then answer the questions following the description.

Introduction: Technically, I was not a beginner in learning this particular skill. I had played a great deal of basketball and had mastered this shot with the right hand, and made attempts with the left, thus, previous experience influenced the learning of the skill. Although the lesson was short, I felt motivation occurred. A man teaching a girl the shot, made me want to do very well to show that girls can learn and do well in sports.

Lesson One: The teacher first directed me to do a few right-handed shots. Then he demonstrated the left-hand lay-up. Next, without the ball, he demonstrated the step-hop-elevate approach and gave verbal directions. He repeated the cue words "step-hop-jump."

After I had practiced this without the ball, he demonstrated the arm motion—no verbal cues were given. Before I tried this, he once again demonstrated the entire lay-up shot. Then he asked me to take the ball and practice pushing it straight up. He had me jump with a one foot take-off and push the ball up and hit the backboard. Again he repeated the demonstration.

I practiced a few more times, with cues being given during the performance or shortly after. There was never any stress on making the goal. Praise was given when my technique was good, whether the shot was made or missed. I kept wanting to use two hands, rather than the one as the teacher wanted. Next, we added steps and dribble—demonstration again, verbal direction was step left, dribble right, step right, shoot. Practice occurred.

Lesson Two: We started by identifying a place on the backboard where the ball could hit and go in. Verbal instruction and demonstration were given by the teacher. I practiced and was made aware of my hand placement idiosyncrasy in technique again. I made a continued effort to change it, but felt awkward.

I continued practice—adding running, passing, and dribbling to the shot. I made a left-handed basket, and the teacher corrected my hand placement. I tried again to make a basket, but was not successful. The class ended with a reminder by the teacher to do some mental practice at home.

a. Was this skill being taught as an open or closed skill?
b. Give an example where negative transfer occurred.
c. Give an example where stress on technique may have interfered with learning.
d. What would you have changed in Lesson One?
e. What would you have changed in Lesson Two?

3. Design a learning environment based on man's sensory, perceptual and motor capacities, and limitations that you feel would enhance the learning of skills.
4. Diagram a model depicting how one learns a movement pattern. Remember, a model is a theoretical explanation as to how something occurs. Apply your model to the teaching situation.

BIBLIOGRAPHY

ADAMS, J. A. Motor skills. *Annual Review of Psychology,* 15:181–202, 1964.

AMMONS, R. B. Effects of knowledge of performance: A survey and tentative theoretical formulation. *Journal of General Psychology,* 54:279–99, 1956.

ANDERSON, J. E. Growth and development today: Implications for physical education. *Social Changes and Sports.* Washington, D.C.: AAHPER, 1958.

ANNETT, J. and H. KAY. Skilled performance. *Occupational Psychology,* 30:112–17, 1956.

————. Knowledge of results and skilled performance. *Occupational Psychology,* 31:69–79, 1957.

————. *Feedback and Human Behavior.* Baltimore: Penguin Books, Inc., 1969.

ARMSTRONG, T. R. Training for the production of memorized movement patterns. NASA Technical Report, No. 26, 1970.

ATKINSON, J. W. The mainsprings of achievement-oriented activity. In J. D. Krumboltz (ed.), *Learning and The Educational Process.* Skokie, Ill.: Rand McNally & Co., 1965.

ATKINSON, J. and D. McCLELLAND. Motivation and behavior. In George H. Litwin and Robert A. Stringer (eds.), *Motivation and Organizational Climate.* Cambridge, Mass.: Division of Research, Graduate School of Business Administration, Harvard University, 1968.

BAHRICK, H. P., M. NOBLE, and P. M. FITTS. Extra task performance as a measure of learning a primary task. *Journal of Experimental Psychology,* 48:198–302, 1954.

BARTLETT, F. C. The measurement of human skill. *Occupational Psychology,* 22:31–38, 1948.

————. *Thinking: An Experimental and Social Study.* New York: Basic Books, 1958.

BERLIN, P. Effects of varied teaching emphases during early learning on acquisition of selected motor skills. *Dissertation Abstracts,* 20, No. 5, 1959.

———— (ed.). A symposium of motor learning. *Quest,* monograph 6, 1966.

BILODEAU, E. A. and I. McD. BILODEAU. Motor skills learning. *Annual Review of Psychology,* 12:243–80, 1961.

BILODEAU, INA McD. Information feedback. In E. A. Bilodeau (ed.), *Acquisition of Skill.* New York: Academic Press, Inc., 1966, pp. 255–96.

BLOOM, B. S., M. D. ENGLEHART, E. J. FURST, W. H. HILL, and D. R. KRATWOHL. *Taxonomy of Educational Objectives: Handbook I: Cognitive Domain.* New York: David McKay Co., Inc., 1956.

BOURNE, L. E. Information feedback. Comments on Professor I. McD. Bilodeau's Paper in Bilodeau E. A. (ed.), *Acquisition of Skill.* New York: Academic Press, Inc., 1966.

BRACKBILL, Y., W. E. BOBLITT, D. DAVLIN, and J. E. WAGNER. Amplihide of response and the delay-retention effect. *Journal of Experimental Psychology*, 66:57–64, 1963.

BRACKBILL, Y., R. B. ISAACA, and N. SMELKINSON. Delay of reinforcement and the retention of unfamiliar, meaningless material. *Psychological Review*, 11:553–54, 1962.

BRACKBILL, Y., J. E. WAGNER, and D. WILSON. Feedback delay and the teaching machine. *Psychology in the Schools*, 1:148–56, 1964.

BROER, M. Effectiveness of a general basic skills curriculum for junior high school girls. *Research Quarterly*, 379:388, 1958.

BRYAN, W. L. and N. HARTER. Studies on the telegraphic language: The acquisition of a hierarchy of habits. *Psychological Review*, 6:345–75, 1899.

BRYDEN, M. P. A model for the sequential organization of behavior. *Canadian Journal Psychological Review*, 21:37–55, 1967.

CHERNIKOFF, R. and F. V. TAYLOR. Reaction time kinesthetic stimulation resulting from sudden arm displacements. *Journal of Experimental Psychology*, 43:1–8, 1952.

COADY, C. The effect of refined principles of kinesthesis in teaching golf skills to college women. Master's Thesis, Indiana University, Bloomington, Indiana, 1950.

COLVILLE, F. M. The learning of motor skills as influenced by knowledge of mechanical principles. *Journal of Education Psychology*, 48:321–27, 1957.

COMBS, A. W. and D. SNYGG. *Individual Behavior*. New York: Harper & Row, Publishers, 1959.

COX, J. W. Some experiments on formal training in the acquisition of skills. *British Journal of Psychology*, 24:67–87, 1933.

CRATTY, B. J. *Movement Behavior and Motor Learning*. Philadelphia: Lea & Febiger, 1964.

CREAMER, L. R. Event uncertainty, psychological refractory period, and human data processing. *Journal of Experimental Psychology*, 66:187–94, 1963.

CROSSMAN, E. R. F. W. A theory of the acquisition of speed-skill. *Ergonomics*, 2:153–66, 1959.

DAVIS, F. Brain training. *Glamour*, Oct., 1970, pp. 170+.

DAVIS, R. The human operation as a single channel information system. *Quarterly Journal of Experimental Psychology*, 9:119–29, 1957.

DIEHL, J. and R. SEIBEL. The relative importance of visual and auditory feedback in speed typewriting. *Journal of Applied Psychology*, 46:365–69, 1962.

DRAZIN, D. H. Effects of foreperiod, foreperiod variability, and probability of stimulus occurrence on simple reaction time. *Journal of Experimental Psychology*, 62:43–50, 1961.

FITTS, P. M. Engineering psychology and equipment design. In S. S. Stevens (ed.), *Handbook of Experimental Psychology*. New York: John Wiley & Sons, Inc., 1951, pp. 1237–1340.

————. The information capacity of the human motor system in controlling the amplitude of movement. *Journal of Experimental Psychology*, 47:381–91, 1954.

————. Perceptual-motor skill learning. In A. W. Melton (ed.), *Categories of Human Learning.* New York: Academic Press, Inc., 1964, pp. 243–85.

————. Factors in complex skill training. In Robert Glasser (ed.), *Training Research and Education.* New York: John Wiley & Sons, Inc., 1965, pp. 177–97.

————. Cognitive aspects of information processing: III. set for speed versus accuracy. *Journal of Experimental Psychology,* 71:849–57, 1966.

———— and M. POSNER. *Human Performance.* Belmont, Calif.: Brooks Cole Publishing Co., 1967.

FOX, P. W. and C. M. LEVY. Acquisition of a simple motor response as influenced by the presence or absence of action visual feedback. *Journal of Motor Behavior,* 1:169–80, 1969.

FLEISHMAN, E. A. and W. E. HEMPEL, JR. The relation between abilities and improvement with practice in a visual discrimination reaction task. *Journal of Experimental Psychology,* 49:301–12, 1955.

————. Comments on human abilities. In E. A. Bilodeau (ed.), *Acquisition of Skill.* New York: Academic Press, Inc., 1966.

FLEISHMAN, E. A. and J. F. PARKER. Use of analytical information concerning task requirements to increase the effectiveness of skill training. *Journal of Applied Psychology,* 45:295–302, 1961.

GAGNE, R. M. and E. A. FLEISHMAN. *Psychology and Human Performance.* New York: Holt, Rinehart & Winston, 1959, pp. 219–62.

GIBBS, G. B. A continuous regulation of skilled responses by kinesthetic feedback. *British Journal of Psychology,* 45:24–39, 1954.

GILMAN, D. A. Feedback prompting and overt correction procedures in non-branching computer assisted instruction programs. *Journal of Educational Research,* 60:423–26, 1967.

GRIFFITH, C. F. An experiment in learning to drive a golf ball. *Athletic Journal,* 11:11, 1931.

HARTSON, L. D. Contrasting approaches to the analysis of skilled movements. *Journal of General Psychology,* 20:263–93, 1939.

HELLEBRANDT, F. A. The physiology of motor learning. *Cerebral Palsy Review,* July–August, 1958.

IRION, A. L. A brief history of research on the acquisition of skill. In E. A. Bilodeau (ed.), *Acquisition of Skill.* New York: Academic Press, Inc., 1966.

JEWETT, A., S. JONES, S. LUNEKE, and S. ROBINSON. Educational Change Through a Taxonomy for Writing Physical Education Objectives. *Quest,* 15, January 1971.

JUDD, C. H. Practice without knowledge of results. *Psychology Research Monograph Supplement,* 7:185–99, 1905.

JUDD, J. H. The Relation of Special Training to General Intelligence. *Education Review,* 36:28–42, 1908.

KAMIJA, J. Conscious control of brain waves. *Psychology Today,* April, 1968.

KIENTZLE, M. J. Properties of learning curves under varied distributions of practice. *Journal of Experimental Psychology,* 36:187–211, 1946.

KNAPP, B. *Skill In Sport, The Attainment of Proficiency.* London: Routledge & Kegan Paul Ltd., 1963.

KRATWOHL, D. R., B. S. BLOOM, and B. B. MASIA. *Taxonomy of Educational Objectives: Handbook II: Affective Domain.* New York: David McKay Co., Inc., 1964.

LANG, P. Autonomic control or learning to play the internal organs. *Psychology Today,* pp. 37+, October 1970.

LASHLEY, K. S. The problem of serial order in behavior. In Lloyd A. Jeffress (ed.), *Cerebral Mechanisms in Behavior, The Hixon Symposium.* New York: John Wiley & Sons, Inc., 1951.

LASHLEY, K. S. and J. BALL. Spinal conduction and kinesthetic sensitivity in the maze habit. *Journal of Comparative Psychology,* 71:105, 1929.

LEIBOWITZ, H. *Visual Perception.* New York: The Macmillan Company, 1965.

LEONARD, G. *Education and Ecstasy.* New York: Delacorte Press, 1968.

LINCOLN, R. A. Learning a rate of movement. *Journal of Experimental Psychology,* 47:465–70, 1954.

MASLOW, A. H. *Motivation and Personality.* New York: Harper & Row, Publishers, 1954.

McGRATH, J. W. The relative importance of kinesthetic and visual cues in learning hand-eye coordination skills. Master's Thesis, University of California, Berkeley, California, 1947.

MELTON, A. W. Implications for a General Theory of Memory. *Journal of Verbal Learning and Verbal Behavior,* 2:1–21, 1963.

——— (ed.). *Categories of Human Learning.* New York: Academic Press, Inc., 1964.

METHENY, E. *Movement and Meaning.* New York: McGraw-Hill Book Company, 1968.

MILLER, G. A. The magical number seven, plus or minus two: Some limits on our capacity for processing information. *Psychological Review,* 63:81–97, 1956.

———, E. GALANTER, and K. PRIBRAM. *Plans and the Structure of Behavior.* New York: Holt, Rinehart & Winston, Inc., 1960.

MILLER, R. B. *Handbook on Training and Equipment Design.* USAF, WADC, Technical Report, No. 53–136, 1953.

MOWRER, O. H. *Learning Theory and the Symbolic Process.* New York: John Wiley & Sons, Inc., 1960.

MUMBY, H. Kinesthetic acuity and balance related to wrestling ability. *Research Quarterly,* 24:327–34, 1953.

NAYLOR, J. C. and G. E. BRIGGS. Long-term retention of learned skills: A review of the literature. ASD Technical Report 61–390, The Ohio State University, 1961.

NEWELL, A., J. C. SHAW, and H. A. SIMON. Elements of a theory of human problem solving. *Psychological Review,* 65:151–66, 1958.

PHILLIPS, M. and D. SUMMERS. Relation of kinesthetic perception to motor learning. *Research Quarterly,* 25:456–69, 1954.

POSNER, M. I. Information reduction in the analysis of sequential tasks. *Psychological Review,* 71:491–504, 1964.

POULTON, E. C. Perceptual anticipation in tracking with two-pointed and one-pointed displays. *British Journal of Psychology,* 43:222–29, 1952.

————. On prediction of skilled movements. *Psychological Bulletin,* 54:467–78, 1957.

PURDY, B. J. and A. LOCKHART. Retention and relearning of gross motor skills after long periods of no practice. *Research Quarterly,* 33:265–72, 1962.

ROGERS, C. and B. F. SKINNER. Some issues concerning the control of human behavior. *Science,* 124, No. 3231:1057–66, Nov. 30, 1956.

ROLOFF, L. Kinesthesis in relation of learning in the selected motor skills. *Research Quarterly,* 24:210–17, 1953.

ROBB, M. Feedback and skill learning. *Research Quarterly,* 39:175–84, 1968.

———— and R. Pew. Skill training for the production of a memorized movement pattern. NASA Contractor Report, 1251, 1968.

ROBB, M. and J. TEEPLE. Video tape and skill learning: An exploratory study. *Educational Technology,* 10:79–82, Nov. 1969.

SASSENRATH, J. M. and C. M. GAVERICK. Effects of differential feedback from examinations on retention and transfer. *Journal of Educational Psychology,* 56:259–63, 1964.

SCOTT, M. G. Measurement of kinesthesis. *Research Quarterly,* 26:324–41, 1955.

SEASHORE, H. and A. BAVELAS. The functioning of knowledge of results in Thorndike's line-drawing experiment. *Psychological Review,* 48:155–64, 1941.

SIMPSON, E. J. The classification of education objectives. *Illinois Teacher of Home Economics,* 10:135–40, Winter, 1966–67.

SINGER, R. *Motor Learning and Human Performance.* New York: The Macmillan Company, 1968.

SLATER-HAMMEL, A. Measurement of kinesthetic perception of muscular force with muscle potential changes. *Research Quarterly,* 28:153–59, 1957.

SMITH, K. U., S. D. ANSELL, J. KOEHLER, G. H. SERVOS, Digital computer system for dynamic analysis of speech and feedback mechanisms. *Journal of the Association for Computing Machinery,* 11:240–51, April, 1964.

SMITH, K. U. and R. SCHAPPE. Feedback analysis of the movement mechanism of handwriting. *The Journal of Experimental Education,* 38:4, Summer, 1970.

SMITH, K. U. and M. F. SMITH. *Cybernetic Principles of Learning and Education.* New York: Holt Rinehart & Winston, Inc., 1966.

SMITH, K. U. and T. J. SMITH. Feedback mechanisms of athletic skill and learning. In Leon E. Smith (ed.), *Psychology of Motor Learning.* Chicago: The Athletic Institute, 1970, pp. 83–195.

SMODE, A. F. Learning and performance in a tracking task under two levels of achievement information feedback. *Journal of Experimental Psychology,* 56:297–304, 1958.

STETSON, R. H. A motor theory of rhythm and discrete succession. *Psychological Review,* 12:150–370, 1905.

———— and J. A. MCDILL. Mechanisms of the different types of movement. *Psychological Monographs,* 32:18–40, 1923.

SULLIVAN, H. J., R. L. BAKER, and R. E. SHULTZ. Effects of intrinsic and extrinsic reinforcement contingencies on learner performance. *Journal of Educational Psychology,* 58:165–67, 1967.

TOFFLER, A. *Future Shock*. New York: Random House, Inc., 1970.

TRAVERS, R. M. W., I. E. REID, and K. R. VAN WAGENEN. Research on reinforcement and its implications for education. *Journal of Teacher Education Journal,* 15:324–29, 1964.

VANEK, M. and B. J. CRATTY. *Psychology and the Superior Athlete,* Toronto: The Macmillan Company, 1970.

VON BUSECK, R. C. Augmented error feedback in a simulated driving task. Unpublished dissertation draft, University of Michigan, 1965.

WAUGH, N. C. and D. A. NORMAN. Primary Memory. *Psychological Review,* 89–104, 1965.

WELFORD, A. P. *Skill and Age*. London: Oxford University Press, 1951.

WHEELER, R. H. and F. T. PERKINS. *Principles of Mental Development*. New York: Crowell Collier and Macmillan, Inc., 1932.

WIEBE, V. R. A study of tests of kinesthesis. *Research Quarterly,* 25:222, 1954.

WIENER, N. W. *Cybernetics*. Cambridge, Mass.: The M.I.T. Press, Copyright 1948, 1961. M.I.T. Paperback Edition published 1965.

WITTE, F. Relation of kinesthetic perception to selected motor skills for elementary school children. *Research Quarterly,* 33:476–84, 1962.

WOODWORTH, R. A. *Experimental Psychology*. New York: Holt Rinehart & Winston, Inc., 1938.

YOUNG, G. A study of kinesthesis in relation to selected movement. *Research Quarterly,* 16:277–87, 1945.

INDEX

A

Ability:
  defined, 17
  general motor, 17
  grouping, 83, 84
  motor, 17
  perceptual-motor, 21
  physical (*see* Physical fitness)
  and success, 16, 17
Adams, J. A., 94
Affective:
  knowledge, 160
  learning, 10–12
Alpha waves, 113
Ammons, R. B., 95
Anderson, J. E., 45
Annett, J., 31, 46, 47, 63, 100
Ansell, J., 98
Anticipation, 49, 133
Armstrong, T. R., 99, 100, 109, 110
Association, theories, 24–28
Asymptote, 13–15
Atkinson, J. W., 82, 83
Audiovisual aids, 58, 59, 70, 71, 150

B

Bahrick, H. P., 54
Ball, J., 104
Bartlett, F. C., 48

Bavelas, A., 106
Behavior:
  assessing, 135–38, 151, 152
  and goals, 33, 34
  terminal, 136, 137
  (*See also* Performance)
Berlin, P., 96
Bilodeau, E. A., 92
Bilodeau, I. MD., 92, 93
Bloom, B., 116, 117
Bourne, L. E., 99
Brackbill, Y., 98
Brain training, 113
Briggs, G. E., 63
Broer, M., 77
Bryan, W. L., 43

C

Central processing system, 40, 41
Chernikoff, R. F., 104
Classification systems:
  abilities and games, 132–34
  levels of difficulty, 129–32
  open-closed continuum, 121–29
  task, 139–41, 145
  traditional, 118–21
Closed skills, 125–27
Coady, C., 103
Cognitive:
  knowledge, 159

Cognitive (*Cont.*)
  learning, 10, 12, 117
  structures, 28
  theories, 28–30
Colville, F. M., 78
Combs, A. W., 28
Communication model, 32, 33
Composite model, 34, 35
Control system model, 33–34
Cox, J. W., 103
Cratty, B. J., 39, 121, 132, 133
Critical components, 138–42
Crossman, E. R. F. W., 14, 15
Cybernetics:
  computor analogy, 4, 41, 42
  and feedback, 31, 102, 104
  and learning, 24
  models, 32–34
  theory, 3, 4, 30–36
Cues:
  auditory, 61
  visual, 59, 60

D

Degeneration, 8, 9
Demonstrations, 52, 59, 60–62
Dependent variable, 11, 12
Detection:
  specificity, 54
  vigilance, 55
Diehl, J., 99
Directions:
  effect on reaction time, 90
Doctrine of prior entry, 54
Drazin, D. H., 87

E

Effectors, 41, 42 (*see also* Learning, effec-
    tive)
Executive program, 43, 44, 46, 47, 51, 52,
    59, 60, 63, 66, 69, 137
Experimental variable, 11, 12
Exteroceptors, 25

F

Feedback:
  action, 94
  arrival time, 97–99
  augmented, 96, 104
  and closed skills, 126
  concurrent, 97–99, 110, 151
  cybernetic theory, 30, 31
  defined, 93

Feedback (*Cont.*)
  dynamic sensory, 93
  error information, 65, 66
  external, 100
  factors affecting, 96–100
  function of, 42
  future of, 111–13
  group interaction, 104
  information, 93
  internal, 100, 103, 104, 126
  intrinsic, 100
  knowledge of results, 92, 93
  and learning, 94
  loops, 100–104
  and motivation, 95
  noise, 105, 106
  on-going process, 64–66
  reference pattern, 106, 107
  removal, 97, 98
  role, 41, 42, 94–96
  and skill learning, 93–115
  social yoking, 104
  and task, 99, 100
  teacher's role, 151
  and teaching, 108, 109, 111, 112
  terminal, 97, 98, 110, 151
  and transfer, 79
  types of movements, 120
Fitts, P. M., 32, 34, 40, 42, 44, 51, 52, 54,
    60, 66, 85, 90, 100, 101, 103, 104, 117,
    128, 129–32, 164, 165
Fleishman, E. A., 17, 18, 165
Form, 69
Fox, P. W., 99

G

Gagne, R. M., 103
Galanter, E., 43
Gestalt psychology, 25, 124
Gibbs, G. B., 104
Gilman, D. A., 105
Goals, 70 (*see also* Executive program)
Goal setting, 79–82, 84
Griffith, C. F., 103

H

Habits, 25, 27
Harter, N., 43
Hartson, L. D., 119
Hellebrandt, F. A., 32
Hempel, W. E., 18
Hierarchical organization, 35, 42, 43, 66,
    67
Homogeneous groupings, 83, 84
Human performance, 3

I

Individual differences, 16
Information:
  amount, 84–86
  bits, 32, 33
  chunks, 32, 33
  decode, 21
  encode, 147
  feedback, 93
  processing, 3, 21, 93, 111
  rate, 84–86
  theory, 32
  types, 147–49
    conservation, 147
    creation, 149
    reduction, 148, 149
Instructional process, 135–54
Interoceptors, 24

J

Jewett, A., 117
Jones, S., 117
Judd, J. H., 77, 78

K

Kamija, J., 113
Kay, H., 46, 47, 63, 100
Kientzle, M. J., 62
Kinesthetic sense (*see* Feedback, internal)
Knapp, B., 39, 121, 124, 127
Koehler, G. H., 98
Kratwohl, D. R., 116

L

Lang, P., 113
Lashley, K. S., 44, 104
Law of effect, 27, 31
Learning:
  conditioning, 26, 27
  contiguity, 26
  curve, 13 (Fig. 1, p. 13)
    plateau, 13–15
  discontinuity, 14
  and feedback, 94, 96
  laws, 27
  measurement, 13, 14
  motor-skill, 10, 12
  rate, 16
  skill, 6, 7
  theories, 23–27
    association, 24–28
    cognitive, 28–30
    cybernetics, 30–36
  types of:
    affective, 11, 12, 16, 117

Learning (*Cont.*)
  cognitive, 10, 12, 117
  effective, 11, 12
  variance, 16
  whole and part, 63, 64
Leibowitz, H., 56
Leonard, G., 112
Level of aspiration, 79–82
Levy, C. M., 99
Lockhart, A., 20
Luneke, S., 117

M

McDill, J. A., 119
McGrath, J. W., 103
Maturation, 8, 9
Melton, A. W., 19, 117
Memory:
  capacity, 19–21, 111
  chunking, 19
  long-term, 19
  of movement patterns, 108–11
  short-term, 19
  span, 19
  theories, 75–77
  (*See also* Retention)
Metheny, E., 113
Miller, G. A., 19, 43
Miller, R. B., 94
Models, 23, 24, 32–35
Motivation:
  achievement, 82, 83
  affects on attention, 58
  cultural influences, 82, 83
  environmental demands, 84, 85
  factor affecting performance, 10
  as feedback, 95, 96
  level of aspiration, 79–82
  task demands, 84, 85
  theories, 79
Motor:
  abilities, 17
  capacity, 15, 16
  skills (*see* Skill)
Motor performance:
  compared with learning, 8, 9
  defined, 7
  factors affecting, 7–10
Movement:
  ballistic, 118, 119
  fixation, 118, 119
  manipulative, 119–21
  memorized patterns, 109, 110
  postural, 119–21
  rapid, 119
  reference patterns, 106–8
  slow, 118, 119

Movement (*Cont.*)
  stereotyped, 122, 125
  transport, 119, 121
Movement time, 90
Mowrer, O. H., 31, 95
Multiplexing (*see* Time sharing)
Mumby, H., 103

N

Naylor, J. C., 63
Neural impulse, 89
Noble, M., 54
Norman, D. A., 19

O

Open skills, 122–24, 127–29
Organismic variables, 7, 8

P

Pacing, 48, 49, 129, 139
Perception:
  defined, 21, 56
  and memory, 20
  process of, 56, 57
Perceptual:
  capacities and limitations, 56–59
  motor abilities, 21
Performance:
  motor, 7
  terminal, 151, 152
Perkins, F. T., 62
Phillips, M. D., 103
Physical fitness, 17 (*see also* Organismic
    variables)
Plan (*see* Executive program)
Plan formation, 52–60
Posner, M. I., 42, 44, 147
Poulton, E. C., 49, 99, 121
Practice:
  modes, 149, 150
  schedules, 62, 63
  and skill acquisition, 60–66
Preprograming, 46
Pribram, K., 43
Proactive inhibition, 75
Proprioceptors, 24, 103
Psychological refractory period, 88
Purdy, B. J., 20

R

Reaction time:
  neural impulse, 89
  tests, 88, 89 (*see* Fig. 6, p. 89)
  variables, 86–90

Receptor:
  capacities and limitations, 53–65
  cues, 61, 62
  (*See also* Skill, mechanisms)
Redundancy, 47
Reference patterns, 106, 107
Reid, I. E., 95
Research, learning, 11
Retention:
  measures, 74, 75
  of motor skills, 76, 77
  (*See also* Memory)
Retroactive inhibition, 75
Robb, M., 71, 109, 110
Robinson, S., 117
Rogers, C., 28, 30
Roloff, L., 103

S

Schappe, R., 98
Schedules of practice, 62, 63
Scott, M. G., 103
Seashore, H., 106
Seible, R., 99
Self-concept, 29, 80
Sensory acuity, 53, 54
Sensory deprivation, 85
Sequential organization, 52, 60, 67–69
Serial organization (*see* Sequential organi-
    zation)
Servomechanisms, 3
Servos, G. H., 98
Simpson, E. J., 117, 156
Singer, R., 25
Single channel hypothesis, 35, 36, 54
Simulation, 149
Skill:
  characteristics, 42–49
  definitions, 1, 2, 38–42
    descriptive, 38, 39
    operational, 38–40
  factors, 74–91
  mechanisms, 40–42 (*see* Fig. 3, p. 41)
  qualities (*see* Skill, characteristics)
  retention, 76, 77
  stages of learning, 51–73
    automatic, 66–72
    plan formation, 53–60
    practice, 60–66
  study, 2, 3
  transfer, 78, 79
  types, 120–29
    closed, 121, 125–27, 128
    open, 121, 122–24, 128
    open-closed, 127–29
  (*See also* Learning)

Skinner, B. F., 25, 30
Slater-Hammel, A., 103
Smith, K. U., 31, 93, 98, 104, 119
Smith, T. J., 93, 119
Smode, A. F., 95
Snygg, D., 28
Speed and accuracy, 85, 86
Sport, classifications, 116–34
Stetson, R. H., 119
Stimulus:
  in association theory, 25
  intensity, 53
  probability, 87
  and response compatibility, 88
Strategy, 69, 70, 72
Subroutines, 43–47, 61, 63, 64, 68, 69, 141,
    142
Summers, D., 103

T

Task:
  analysis, 64, 138, 144–46
  critical components, 138–42
  demands, 84–86
  and feedback, 99, 100, 110, 111
Task requirements, 9
Taylor, F. V., 104
Taxonomy:
  criteria, 117, 118
  Fitts's, 129–32
  Knapp's, 121–28
  Simpson's, 156–58

Taxonomy (*Cont.*)
  Vanek and Cratty's, 132–34
  (*See also* Classification system)
Teeple, J., 71
Temporal patterning, 47, 48, 60, 61, 66,
    72
Time sharing, 54, 55
Toffler, A., 113
Transfer:
  general patterns, 28, 77, 78
  identical elements, 28, 77
  and skill acquisition, 78, 79
Travers, R. M. W., 95

V

Vanek, M., 121, 132, 133
VanWagenen, K. R., 95
VonBuseck, R. C., 96

W

Waugh, N. C., 19
Wheeler, R. H., 62
Whole and part learning, 63, 64, 126
Wiebe, V. R., 103
Wiener, N. W., 30, 92, 93
Witte, F., 103
Woodworth, R. A., 46

Y

Young, G. A., 103